1 MONTH OF FREE READING

at

www.ForgottenBooks.com

By purchasing this book you are eligible for one month membership to ForgottenBooks.com, giving you unlimited access to our entire collection of over 1,000,000 titles via our web site and mobile apps.

To claim your free month visit:

www.forgottenbooks.com/free917325

* Offer is valid for 45 days from date of purchase. Terms and conditions apply.

ISBN 978-0-266-97007-1
PIBN 10917325

This book is a reproduction of an important historical work. Forgotten Books uses state-of-the-art technology to digitally reconstruct the work, preserving the original format whilst repairing imperfections present in the aged copy. In rare cases, an imperfection in the original, such as a blemish or missing page, may be replicated in our edition. We do, however, repair the vast majority of imperfections successfully; any imperfections that remain are intentionally left to preserve the state of such historical works.

Forgotten Books is a registered trademark of FB &c Ltd.
Copyright © 2018 FB &c Ltd.
FB &c Ltd, Dalton House, 60 Windsor Avenue, London, SW19 2RR.
Company number 08720141. Registered in England and Wales.

For support please visit www.forgottenbooks.com

SIXTH ANNUAL REPORT

OF THE

PRESIDENT OF HARVARD UNIVERSITY

TO

THE OVERSEERS

ON

THE STATE OF THE INSTITUTION,

FOR THE ACADEMICAL YEAR

1830–31.

CAMBRIDGE:
E. W. METCALF AND COMPANY,
Printers to the University.
1832.

To the Honorable and Reverend,
  the Board of Overseers of Harvard University.

The President of that Seminary, in conformity with the directions of the Board, respectfully presents the following

REPORT.

THE general relations of the several departments of the University, during the last academic year, will appear by the specifications in the Appendix.

By comparing these specifications with those of the last Annual Report, it will be seen that few alterations, and none very material, have been found necessary in the course of studies, or in the general arrangements of the University.

The plan of studies adopted in January, 1830, has been successfully pursued; and the advantages anticipated from the changes then introduced, have been attained.

So far as depends upon general regulations, the best assurance for the continued and unremitted attention of students to their exercises, will be found in the certainty that at every recitation each individual will be examined; and that the estimate of scholastic rank must depend, not upon occasional brilliant success, but upon the steady, uniform, and satisfactory performance of each exercise.

The effect of these principles, and of others of a similar tendency, is already, it is apprehended, seen in the increased and, it is believed, increasing attention to the course of studies of the University, and also in the proficiency and good moral conduct of the members of the institution. In these respects the President deems himself authorized to represent to the Overseers, that the state of the University has been, during the past year, in a high degree satisfactory.

The specifications in the Appendix, under the head of "Omissions and Punishments," will exhibit all the exceptions, which have occurred, to the above statement, as well as the remedies the Faculty of the University have seen fit to apply.

Among these specifications, it will be found that several individuals have been separated from the University for want of attention to their studies, sometimes by advice given to parents to that effect, and sometimes by a direct application of the power relative to matriculation vested in the Faculty by the laws of the University. The exercise of this power, in its nature always delicate, and often difficult, is, in fact, indispensable to success in the attempt to elevate the standard of intellectual attainment in seminaries of learning. So long as, through fear of giving pain to parents, or through a desire of having the reputation of numbers, this power is left unexercised, the inducements to continued and efficient attention to study are essentially diminished.

In addition to a strict enforcement of the course of studies established in the University, an enlarged sphere of action has been opened for the encouragement of the spirit of voluntary study; not only by the facilities and inducements held out for the pursuit of the modern languages, beyond what the general laws of the University require, but also, recently, by the establishment of a philological department, for teaching the theory and practice of instruction, under the superintendence of

Dr. Beck in the Latin, and Mr. Felton in the Greek department.

The object of this recent institution is not only highly interesting to all those, who wish to become more thoroughly acquainted with the learned languages than the usual limits of the academic course permit, but must be peculiarly advantageous to all those who propose to make instruction the business of their lives; and is particularly adapted to give to the community, in the course of time, well instructed and efficient teachers of youth in our seminaries of learning. The institution can be considered, at present, in the light only of an experiment. It has commenced however under very favorable auspices. Five and twenty members of the Senior Class, and six Resident Graduates, have voluntarily taken upon themselves the duties it enjoins. As soon as the general arrangements of the University permit, it is also contemplated to add the Mathematics to the studies of this department.

The condition of the Library of the University, its state of exposure to fire, the impossibility of obtaining indemnity for its loss by any amount of insurance, and, considering the nature, scarceness, and value of a portion of its contents, the absolute irretrievableness of such loss, should it occur, are so generally known, that it may seem unnecessary to add any thing to the suggestions made on these topics on former occasions. The greatness of the interest, however, and the existing, and daily increasing, importance of the relations of this library, will not justify silence on the subject.

The Library of the University now consists of *forty thousand volumes.* Nominally it belongs to Harvard University. Virtually, and to every beneficial purpose, it is the property of the Commonwealth. Learned men, engaged in useful works in any part of the state, have free access to it for any use connected with the objects of their pursuit. It cannot be questioned, that its destruction would sensibly affect the state of general intelligence and the progress of science in the Commonwealth, and create a want of facilities for the diffusion of knowledge, which the wealth and exertions of half a century could not effectually supply. Very many of the works it contains, if lost, could not be replaced. In some of them the libraries of Europe are now deficient.

In the recent controversy between the United States and England relative to the boundaries of the state of Maine, maps and works highly important, and, in the opinion of the counsel of the United States, in some respects conclusive in favor of the right of the United States, were found in this library, which could not be obtained elsewhere, either in Europe or America; and as such, the use of them was solicited by the general government, and granted by the Corporation, for the purpose of sending them with the American Commissioners to Europe, in support of the claims of the United States.

By the munificence of private individuals, the department of the Library relative to American history is unrivalled both in extent and completeness. The same may be said concerning the collection of maps and charts. In respect to each of these departments of science, it has no competitor on the continent of America; — perhaps none in the world.

The use of its treasures is opened with a liberality that is limited only by the necessity, which requires them essentially to be at the command of the students in the University, and of the several literary men or learned associations connected with it, or residing or established in its immediate vicinity. Specific provisions, however, exist and are daily acted upon, by which persons engaged in useful works, in any part of the Commonwealth, are permitted to have the use of any books, which are important to their researches, and which cannot be obtained elsewhere. It is scarcely possible for any library to be more truly *public* than that of this institution.

The Library has now increased to a size, for which the building at present appropriated to its accommodation is wholly inadequate. Not only every space in all the alcoves is completely occupied, but ranges of shelves have been necessarily constructed in the centre of the several rooms; and so fill the area of those rooms as to render their occupation for any general purpose either extremely inconvenient or impracticable.

From these circumstances the books themselves are rendered also liable to great injury and loss. Unless placed in alcoves properly secured, and inaccessible except to responsible and licensed persons, no library can be safe from damage and even loss, both from accident and design. In the present necessarily exposed situation of these books, it is absolutely impossible to attain the requisite security against such injuries. Some have already been ascertained; more must hereafter, in all probability, take place.

In addition to these circumstances let it be remembered, that this library, thus valuable and thus unrivalled on this continent, is deposited in a building almost in immediate contact with another, in which there are, every winter, more than *thirty fires*, under the care, for the most part, of young men, liable to be called, all at the same time, from their rooms, four or five times a day, to their meals or their recitations; and to be absent from them for an hour, and sometimes for two hours, at a time. It is impossible for any one, in the daily knowledge and observation of these facts, not to feel a deep and urgent solicitude upon the subject.

The President of the University cannot, therefore, deem his duty discharged, without pressing upon the Overseers of this ancient seminary, both as public and as literary men, the obligation of not permitting this important interest any longer to remain exposed to such great and obvious hazard.

The Corporation of the University have no means applicable to the erection of such a building as the exigency of the Library requires. They have no other resource than public liberality.

It seems scarcely possible, that in a Commonwealth distinguished for its fostering care of literature, and under circumstances of uncommon public prosperity, an appeal to that liberality on a subject of so plain and impressive general concern, — so extensive in its nature and so permanent in its consequences, — should not be met with a spirit corresponding to the importance of the object and the urgency of the circumstances which occasion the appeal.

All which is respectfully submitted by

JOSIAH QUINCY, { President of Harvard University.

Cambridge, 6 January, 1832.

APPENDIX.

A.

DEPARTMENT OF THEOLOGY.

THIS, during the past year, has been exclusively under the superintendence of the Rev. Henry Ware, D. D., Hollis Professor of Divinity.

This branch was pursued in the first term of the Junior year, on Tuesdays, Thursdays, and Saturdays, from X to XII, A. M. This extended through the first term, the Class being heard in Divisions an hour each, and was continued through the first four weeks of the second term.

In the first term, the study of Paley's Evidences of Christianity commenced, and was pursued in recitations, three hours per week, by lessons of about ten pages each, until the beginning of November, by which time this book was finished. The Class then entered upon the study of Butler's Analogy; the first part of which was finished by the end of the first term. About four weeks of the second term were occupied by this Class in reviewing Paley and Butler, after which, instruction in the branch closed for the Junior year.

In the second term, the Seniors commenced this branch; and Lectures on the New Testament were given to the whole Class by the Professor three times a week, *viz.*, on Mondays, Tuesdays, and Wednesdays, for one hour each day at the second hour before the prayer bell in the afternoon. The exercise included Questions on the Lecture.

Instruction in this branch closed with this term. — Besides the duties above enumerated, Dr. Ware performs the Chapel morning and evening services alternately with the Rev. Henry Ware, jun. The Sabbath services are performed one half by him, and the other half by the Rev. Henry Ware, jun. and the Rev. John Gorham Palfrey.

B.

DEPARTMENT OF MORAL PHILOSOPHY, CIVIL POLITY, AND POLITICAL ECONOMY.

Levi Hedge, LL. D., Alford Professor of Natural Religion, Moral Philosophy, and Civil Polity, is at present the head of this department. From circumstances connected with the state of his health, his services during the last six months have been dispensed with. The department during that period was conducted satisfactorily by George S. Hillard, one of the Proctors of the University.

Instruction in this branch was conducted through studies and recitations in Stewart's Elements of the Philosophy of the Mind; Paley's Moral Philosophy; Brown's Philosophy of the Human Mind, abridged by Dr. Hedge; Say's Political Economy; and Rawle on the Constitution of the United States.

These studies commenced with the Junior year, in Stewart's Elements; the first volume of which the Class finished about the middle of October. After this they entered upon Paley's Moral Philosophy, which they finished by the end of the first term. After the end of the first term, the Juniors did not recite in these branches during that year.

Junior Year.

Instruction commenced with the first term, the Class being heard in Divisions;

   1st Division, after Prayers, A. M.
   2d   do.   at Study Bell, do.

every day in the week, to the end of the term.

Forensics every other week, on Friday, occupied three hours before the evening prayers, alternating with the Seniors.

In the Senior year instruction in this branch was recommenced, with Brown's Treatise on the Mind. Both volumes of this work were finished by the sixth or seventh week of the second term. The Class then entered upon Say's Political Economy, which was finished by about the eighth week in the third term. Rawle on the Constitution then succeeded in the course, and with it instruction in this branch ceased.

The Class were taught in Divisions;

   1st Division, at 2d hour before Prayers, P. M.
   2d   do.   1st   do.   do.   do.

four days in the week.

In the second and third terms it was also taught in Divisions;

   1st Division, after Prayers, A. M.
   2d   do.   at Study Bell, do.

Forensics every other Friday, alternating with the Juniors, for three hours before evening prayers.

C.

DEPARTMENT OF MATHEMATICS AND NATURAL PHILOSOPHY.

This, during the past year, has been under the superintendence of John Farrar, A. M., Hollis Professor of Mathematics and Natural Philosophy; assisted by Seth Sweetser, Tutor, who exclusively instructed the Freshman Class, and by Joel Giles, A. B., and Thomas Hopkinson, A. B., Proctors, who exclusively instructed the Sophomore Class, in this department.

Instruction in this branch commenced in *the Freshman year*, with recitations from the " Cambridge Mathematics," beginning with Plane Geometry, which was completed in the first term. To this the study of Algebra succeeded. This was finished by the end of the second term; and by the end of the Freshman year, the Class finished the study of Solid Geometry.

Instruction was continued in *the Sophomore year*, by recitations in the Application of Algebra to Geometry; to which Trigonometry succeeded, then Topography, and then Fluxions. With these, instruction in Pure Mathematics terminated, about the end of the Sophomore year.

To the above course of Pure Mathematics, succeeded instruction in Natural Philosophy, commencing with the second term of *the Junior Year;* this Class having no instruction in this department during the first term. The Juniors entered upon the study of Mechanics at the beginning, and finished it about the end, of the second term.

Instruction was given in this branch to the Junior Class in the third term; — 1. In Electricity. 2. In Magnetism. 3. In Electro-Magnetism. 4. In Optics. In the text-book of this branch, they advanced, on this last topic, about fifty pages by the end of the Junior year.

Instruction in Natural Philosophy was continued, during the first term of *the Senior Year*, by recitations every morning in the week, and on Tuesdays and Thursdays in the forenoon, and by lectures once a week, besides five evening lectures.

All the instruction in this branch terminated with the first term of the Senior year, with the exception of the lectures.

In the Freshman Year.

The Class was heard in Sections every day in the week, except Saturday, allowing one hour to each Section; and if the Instructer saw fit, he divided the hour between *demisections*, allowing half an hour to each.

Heard by the Tutor.
{ 1st Section from 10 to 11.
  2d   "   "   11 to 12.
  3d   "   in the 2d hour before P. M. Prayers.
  4th   "   in the 1st "   "   "   " }

Five hours a week (for 40 weeks) to each Student is 5 × 40 = 200 hours, and 200 lessons for the Freshman year.

The time required of Instructors is 4 × 200 = 800 hours.

In the Sophomore Year.

The Class was heard in Sections, four days in the week, viz. on Tuesdays, Thursdays, Fridays, and Saturdays, at the following hours, viz.

On Tuesdays and Thursdays.

1st Proctor. { 1st Section heard in the 2d hour before P. M. Prayers.
               2d   "   "   "   1st hour   "   "   " }

2d Proctor. { 3d   "   "   "   2d hour   "   "   "
               4th   "   "   "   1st hour }

On Fridays.

1st Proctor. { 1st Section heard from 10 to 11, A. M.
               2d   "   "   "   11 to 12, " }

2d Proctor. { 3d   "   "   "   10 to 11, "
               4th   "   "   "   11 to 12, " }

On Saturdays.

1st Proctor. { 1st Section heard in the hour after A. M. Prayers.
               2d   "   "   "   at Study Bell. }

2d Proctor. { 3d   "   "   "   in the hour after A. M. Prayers.
               4th   "   "   "   at Study Bell. }

Four hours to each Student is 4 × 40 = 160 hours, or 160 lessons for the Sophomore year; occupying *an hour for each* Section.

The time required of Instructors in 4 × 160 = 640 hours.

In the Junior Year.

First term, no instruction in this branch.

Second and third terms.

Heard by Professor. { 1st Section, after A. M. Prayers, $\frac{3}{4}$ hour.
                      2d   "   "   "   " $\frac{3}{4}$ " }

Heard by Tutor.   { 3d   "   "   "   " $\frac{3}{4}$ "
                      4th   "   "   "   " $\frac{3}{4}$ " }

viz. $4\frac{1}{2}$ hours for each Section or Student × 25 = $112\frac{1}{2}$ hours, or 150 lessons.

Time required of Instructors 4 × $112\frac{1}{2}$ = 450.

APPENDIX.

Besides the above, the Professor gave a lecture to the whole Class, from 11 to 12, on Mondays, Tuesdays, Wednesdays, and Thursdays, of the third term.

In the Senior Year.

Instruction in this branch ends with the first term.

First Term.

Heard by Professor. { 1st Section, after A. M. Prayers, $\frac{3}{4}$ hour.
2d " " " " $\frac{3}{4}$ "
Heard by Tutor. { 3d " " " " $\frac{3}{4}$ "
4th " " " " $\frac{3}{4}$ "

Besides the above, two Recitations were given weekly, on Tuesdays and Thursdays, to this Class, from 10 to 12; viz. $5\frac{1}{2}$ hours weekly for each Student $\times 15 = 82\frac{1}{2}$, or 120 lessons.

The time required of Instructers $4 \times 82\frac{1}{2} = 330$ hours.

General Result.

Freshmen — Each Student occupied in 200 Lessons 200, and Instructers 800
Sophomores — " " 160 " 160, " 640
Juniors — " " 150 " $112\frac{1}{2}$, " 450
Seniors — " " 120 " $82\frac{1}{2}$, " 330

Whole No. of Lessons in Coll. Course 630   hours 555,   hours 2220

The first term, the Professor heard the
1st Section of Seniors $\frac{3}{4}$ of an hour, after Prayers, A. M.
2d " " $\frac{3}{4}$ " " " "

$1\frac{1}{2}$ hours every day.

The Tutor heard the

3d Section of Seniors $\frac{3}{4}$ of an hour, after Prayers, A. M.
4th " " $\frac{3}{4}$ " " " "

$1\frac{1}{2}$ hours every day.

Second and third terms the Juniors were heard in the same way.

The Tutor also heard every day the

1st Section of Freshmen from 10 to 11.
2d " " " " 11 to 12.
3d " " " " 2d hour before Prayers, P. M.
4th " " " " 1st " " " "

The *first Proctor* heard on Tuesdays and Thursdays

1st Section of Sophomores at 2d hour before Prayers, P. M.
2d " " " 1st " " " "

On Fridays,

1st Section of Sophomores from 10 to 11.
2d   "   "   "   " 11 to 12.

On Saturdays,

1st "   "   "   immediately after Prayers, A. M.
2d   "   "   "   at Study Bell.

The *second Proctor* heard, on Tuesdays and Thursdays,

3d Section of Sophomores at 2d hour before Prayers, P. M.
4th   "   "   "   1st "   "   "   "

On Fridays,

3d   "   "   "   from 10 to 11.
4th "   "   "   " 11 to 12.

On Saturdays.

3d   "   "   "   immediately after Prayers, A. M.
4th "   "   "   at Study Bell.

The Professor heard two sections of the Seniors in the first, and of the Juniors in the second and third terms, 1¼ hours every day in the week, or 9 hours weekly, equal to annual labor of 360 hours; and in the first term he gave two recitations to the Seniors, of two hours each week, or five hours weekly; and to the Juniors one lecture of an hour, but divided among four days, in the third term.

The Tutor heard two Sections of the Seniors in the first, and of the Juniors in the second and third terms, after morning prayers . . . . 1¼ hours
    And the Freshmen   4

Daily . . . . . 5¼ hours.
Number of Days in the week . 5

Hours, weekly . . 27¼ hours.
Saturday Morning   1¼

Weekly . . 29 hours.
Weeks in the Year . 40

Hours for the Tutor   1160

The first Proctor heard the Sophomores two hours for four days in the week, or . . . 8 hours weekly.
40
———
320
The second Proctor, as above, the same . . } 320 "
———
Hours of service by Proctors 640
Professor's occupation in recitation with Seniors and Juniors. } 9 × 40 = 360
4 × 15 = 60
420 hours.
" " in lectures to the Seniors in the first term } 1 × 15 = 15
evening lec. 5
" " in lectures to the Juniors in the third term } 4 × 13 = 52
evening lec. 4
———
76
Time stated by the Professor as employed in preparing for lectures . } 228
———
Total of Professor's occupation . . 724 hours.
Total of Professor's occupation in recitation . } . 420 hours.
" Tutor's occupation . 1160 "
" Proctors' " . . 640 "
———
In recitations . 2220 hours.
In lectures . . 304 "
———
Total occupation of Instructers in recitations and lectures . . } 2524 hours.

Any excess of occupation above assigned to the Tutor beyond that assigned to the Professor, being reduced by the coming of the latter in aid of the former, at such times as was found convenient or deemed reasonable.

D.

DEPARTMENT OF RHETORIC AND ORATORY.

This is, at present, under the superintendence of Edward T. Channing, A. M., Boylston Professor of Rhetoric and Oratory; assisted in the latter by Jonathan Barber, M. D.

Instruction in reading and declamation was given to *the Freshman Class*, every day in the week through the first half of the year by Dr. Barber; the Class being heard by sections. Two sections attending every alternate week, after morning prayers. Each section having three exercises in reading or declamation every week. In the latter half of the year it was thought that Dr. Barber's services might be more advantageously directed to the Senior and Junior Classes, and they were accordingly so applied.

In the *Sophomore year*, the Class, under the instruction of the Professor, commenced Lowth's Grammar in the first term, and finished it in about *nine weeks*, at the rate of ten pages an exercise. To Lowth succeeded Blair's Lectures, which the Class finished in about *twenty weeks*, at the rate of one lecture an exercise. The study of Hedge's Logic followed. This was finished by the end of the year, at the rate of about twelve pages the lesson.

The Sophomores attended the Professor in the above studies on Mondays and Wednesdays from 10 to 12 A. M., and were heard in sections half an hour each, during the whole year; and also attended with Themes at the Study Bell, from one to two hours, as was found necessary, every Saturday. The Class bringing in their Themes by divisions every week, a division each week at the Study Bell.

In addition to the above the Professor attended to the hearing of the Sophomore Class in either reading or declamation one hour, four days in the week, after morning prayers; two sections attending alternately; each section having three exercises in reading or declamation every week.

In the *Junior Year* instruction was given in this branch wholly through the medium of themes, lectures, readings, and declamations.

Themes were delivered in by this Class every other Friday (the intermediate Friday being reserved for Forensics) in the three hours preceeding prayers in the afternoon.

Twenty lectures on Rhetoric were given in the second term of this year, on Tuesdays and Thursdays, at 11 o'clock.

Dr. Barber heard this Class either in reading or declamation in sections on four days of the week, an hour being given to each section.

In the *Senior Year* this branch was conducted wholly through the medium of themes and declamations; each of which occupied a like time, and was conducted in the same manner by the respective instructers, as is above specified in relation to the Junior year.

In the Sophomore, Junior, and Senior classes, each student delivered *twenty* themes each year; *one* for the examining committee.

In addition to the above Dr. Barber was engaged to deliver a public lecture to all the classes once a week on Elocution; which he did as frequently as was found expedient.

Time occupied by the Exercises under the care of the Professor.

Sophomores.

80 Recitations, 2 hours each	160 hours.
150 Exercises in reading and speaking, 1 hour each,	150
38 Exercises in composition, 1½ hours each .	57

Juniors.

19 Exercises in composition, 2½ hours each .	48
19 Lectures with examinations, 1 hour each .	19

Seniors.

18 Exercises in composition 2½ hours each .	45
Seniors and Juniors 40 Exercises in declamation, 1 hour each	40
Time occupied in correcting 56 sets of Themes, between 7 and 8 hours each, say . .	430
Two Examinations of a Class before the committee	10
	959

The Professor also inspects the Performances, about 60 in number, for the four public exhibitions.

E.

DEPARTMENT OF GREEK.

This is at present under the superintendence of the Rev. John S. Popkin, D. D., Eliot Professor of Greek Literature; assisted by Cornelius C. Felton, A. M., Tutor.

Instruction in Greek commences with the *Freshman Class*, in Dalzel's Collectanea Majora.

They recite, during that year, about 274 pages of volume first, and 80 pages of volume second. These they also review in the course of the year. Besides which they have a Sunday lesson, recited every Monday morning, of about five pages of Griesbach's New Testament, beginning with the Acts. On Saturday morning the Class are heard in Greek Grammar or Roman Antiquities.

Instruction in this branch is continued in the *Sophomore year*, commencing with Sophocles in the Collectanea; the second volume of which is finished, as also that part of the first volume, which was omitted in the Freshman year, with a review of all the lessons recited this year. In this year the recitations are all in the regular Classics.

Instruction, in this branch, in the *Junior year*, is continued with the Iliad, eleven or twelve books of which will probably be read and

APPENDIX.

reviewed by the end of the second term. In the third term the Iliad will be continued and reviewed; or Demosthenes de Coronâ.

There is, between the studies of the Greek and Latin Languages, an alternation through the whole college course of instruction in those branches. Two sections recite one week in Latin while the others recite in Greek, and so alternately.

In the Freshman Year.

Half the Class is heard the first five days of the week, in sections.

1st Section after Prayers, A. M.	.	1 hour.
2d " at Study Bell "	.	1 "
1st " at 2d hour before Prayers, P.M.		1 "
2d " at 1st hour " " "		1 "

4 hours.

Greek 20 hours.

On Saturdays.

1st Section, Greek Grammar or Antiquities	.	1 hour.
2d " " "	. .	1 "

For the Student 11 hours per week. — For the Instructer 22 hours.
   (weeks) 20   (weeks) 40 "

      220   Whole year   880 hours.

In the Sophomore year.

On Mondays, Wednesdays, and Fridays.

1st Section after Prayers, A. M.	. . . .	1 hour.
2d " at Study Bell "	. . .	1 "

2 hours.

On Tuesdays and Thursdays.

1st Section after Prayers, A. M.	. . . .	1 hour.
2d " at Study Bell "	. . . .	1 "
1st " from 10 o'clock to 11	. . . .	1 "
2d " " 11 " to 12	. . . .	1 "

4 hours.

viz. for each Student 1 hour for 3 days — for Instructer 2 hours.

" " "	1 × 3 = 3 hours		6
" " "	2 for 2 = 4 "		8
" " "	per week 7 hours,	for Inst.	14 hours.
	20		40

Occupation for each Student } 140 hours.   For } 560 hours.
for Sophomore year   Inst. }

In the Junior year.

On Mondays, Tuesdays, Wednesdays, and Thursdays.
1st Section at 2d hour before P. M. Prayers . 1 hour.
2d "   at 1st "   "   "   1 "
                                     ―
                                     2

viz. for each Student 1 hour for 4 days — for Instructer 2 hours for 4 days.

Equal to 4 hours weekly   "   8 h. weekly.
          20   40

Occupation for each Student in Junior year } 80 hours. Occupation for Instructer } 320 } hours for the year.

General Result.

In Freshman year, for Student 220 hours—for Instructer 880 hours.
   Sophomore "   "   140 "   "   560 "
   Junior   "   "   80 "   "   320 "

Total for the Student 440   For Instructers 1760 hours.

Arranged between the present instructers, the labor is as follows:

The Professor attends Freshmen exclusively, viz.   880 hours.

For the Tutor — Monday and Wednesday.

1st Section of Sophomores after Prayers, A. M.   1 hour.
2d   "   "   at Study Bell, "   1 "
1st "   Juniors   2d hour before Prayers, P. M. 1 "
2d   "   " -   1st "   "   "   "   1 "
                                                   ―
                  2 days—4 hours   4 hours.

Tuesday and Thursday.

1st Section of Sophomores after Prayers, A. M.   1 hour.
2d   "   "   at Study Bell, "   1 "
1st "   "   from 10 to 11, "   1 "
2d   "   "   from 11 to 12, "   1
1st "   Juniors   2d hour before Prayers P. M. 1 "
2d   "   "   1st "   "   "   "   1 "
                                                   ―
                  2 days—6 hours   6 hours.

Friday.

1st Section of Sophomores after Prayers, A. M.   1 hour.
2d   "   "   at Study Bell, "   1 "
                                                   ―
                  1 day—2 hours   2 hours.

```
2 days—4 hours =  8 hours
2   "    6  "   = 12   "
1   "    2  "   =  2   "
                ────────
                22 hours
                40
                ────────
               880 hours for the Tutor.
```

The Professor prefers to instruct the Freshman Class, with the consent of the Tutor and the Faculty, on account of the nature and arrangement of the studies, in connexion with his other duties. He gives Lectures on Greek Literature at times found convenient.

F.

DEPARTMENT OF LATIN.

This is at present, and has been during the greater part of the last year, under the superintendence of Charles Beck, J. U. D., instructer in the Latin language, assisted by Henry S. McKean, A. M., Tutor.

Instruction in this branch commenced in the *Freshman year*, with Folsom's Selections from Livy. These were finished at the end of the first term. The study of Horace succeeded, and continued through the Freshman year. Each recitation embraced about four pages, both in Livy and Horace. On Monday morning *Grotius de Veritate Religionis Christianæ*, and on Saturday morning Roman Antiquities, were recited by this Class.

The *Sophomores* began with Tacitus. They finished his History, at the rate of about five pages a lesson, about the end of the first term. The class then commenced *Excerpta* from *Cicero* and *Quintilian*, which they finished and reviewed, by the middle of the third term. They then commenced with Tacitus *de Moribus Germaniæ*, and having finished this, they proceeded to his *Life of Agricola*.

The *Junior year* commenced with Juvenal, which was finished by the end of the first term in this year.

In the second term, the Class reviewed and continued the study of the *Annals;* and with this work the Junior year closed, and all study of the Latin language, by the Junior Class, terminated in the University.

Half the Class was heard the first five days of the week in sections, alternating weekly with the other half in Greek.

APPENDIX. xiii

In the Freshman Year.

3d Section heard after Prayers, A. M.		1 hour.
4th " " at Study Bell, "		1 "
3d " " from 10 o'clock to 11		1 "
4th " " " 11 " to 12		1 '

                                                                          4 hours.
                                  Latin   5
                                                   20

On Saturdays.

3d Section heard in Roman Antiquities	1 hour.
4th " " " " "	1 "
To each Student 11 hours per week—To Instructers	22 hours.
20	40
220 " for the year— "	880 hours.

In consequence of the alternations between the Latin and Greek branches, the recitations, as to the Student, occupy only one fourth of the time required of the Instructers in these branches.

In the Sophomore Year.

On Mondays, Wednesdays, and Fridays.

3d Section after Prayers, A. M.	1 hour.
4th " at Study Bell, "	1
	2 hours.

On Tuesdays and Thursdays.

3d Section after Prayers, A. M.	1 hour.
4th " at Study Bell, "	1 "
3d " from 10 to 11, "	1 "
4th " from 11 to 12, "	1 '
	4

For each Student 1 hour for 3 days—for Instructer 2 hours for 3 days = 6 h.
                                               3
"   2 h. for 2 days = 4 h.   "   "   4 hours for 2 days = 8 h.

Weekly occupation for Stud. 7 h.—for Instructer . . . . 14 h.
                                      20   40

Occupation for each Stnd. } 140 hours.   For the Instructer 560 h.
for Sophomore year

APPENDIX.

In the Junior Year.

On Mondays, Tuesdays, Wednesdays, and Thursdays.

3d Section at 2d hour before Prayers, P. M.			1 hour.
4th " 1st " " "			1 "

2 hours

viz. for each Student 1 hour for 4 days.—For Instructer   2 "
                                                                         4

4 h. weekly   "   8 hours.
     20   40

Occupation for the Student in the Junior year } 80 hours.   Occupation for the Instructer. } 320 hours.

General Result.

In Freshman year, for Student 220 hours.   For Instructers 880 hours.
     Sophomore "   "   140 "   "   "   560 "
     Junior   "   "   80 "   "   "   320 "

Total for the Student   440 hours.   Total for Instructers 1760 hours.

Arranged between the present Instructers, the labor is as follows.

Tutor attends Freshmen exclusively, viz.   880 hours.

For the Professor—Monday and Wednesday.

1st Section of Sophomores after Prayers, A. M.		1 hour.
2d " " " at Study Bell, "		1 "
1st " Juniors 2d hour before Prayers, P. M.		1 "
2d " " " 1st " " "		1 "

2 days—4 hours   4 hours.

Tuesday and Thursday.

1st Section of Sophomores after Prayers, A. M.		1 hour.
2d " " " at Study Bell, "		1 "
1st " " " from 10 to 11, "		1 "
2d " " " " 11 to 12, "		1 "
1st " Juniors 2d hour before Prayers, P. M.		1 "
2d " " " " " " "		1 "

2 days—6 hours   6 hours.

Friday.

1st Section of Sophomores after Prayers, A. M.		1 hour.
2d " " " at Study Bell, "		1 "

2 hours.

```
2 days—4 hours=  8 hours.
2  "    6  "   = 12  "
1  "    2  "   =  2  "
```

Labor of the Professor   22 hours, weekly
                         40 "   or for the year =   880 hours.
    Tutor attends the Freshmen exclusively,   .   880 "
                                                  ————
                                                  1760 hours.

G.

DEPARTMENT OF CHEMISTRY AND MINERALOGY.

This is at present under the superintendence of John W. Webster, M. D., Erving Professor of Chemistry and Mineralogy.

During the first, and part of the second term, the Erving Professor is occupied in giving lectures in the Medical School, to the medical students four months, including the winter vacation.

Instruction in Chemistry begins with the *Juniors*, as soon after the commencement of the second term as the Medical Lectures close in Boston, and continues on Tuesdays, Thursdays, and Saturdays, at 10 o'clock, A. M., through the term, ending about the middle of the third term. The Seniors have liberty to attend.

The *Seniors* commence the study of Mineralogy about the middle of the third term, as soon as the Professor has finished Chemistry with the Juniors, commencing at the 2d hour before the prayer bell in the afternoon, and extending through the Senior year.

In respect of time, Dr. Webster gives in Chemistry, when the study is pursued by the Juniors in the second term, — for 8 weeks, 2 recitations, of an hour each, in the week, or   .   .   16 recitations.

And 3 lectures a week for half the time,
or four weeks, being   .   .   .   12
    2 do.   do   do.   8
                                  ——
        Of an hour each   .   .   .   .   20 lectures.
                                          ——
                                          36

And in the third term he is occupied one hour every day in teaching Mineralogy, giving 59 lectures, ...   59 lectures.
                                          ——
            Lectures and Recitations   95

In addition to which, he states, that from 5 to 8 hours are occupied by him in preparations for each lecture, in cleaning and replacing the apparatus, and taking down and replacing the minerals used in each lecture. He is also much occupied in making additions to the cabinet, by collecting specimens, and making exchanges, at home and abroad.

Besides the above, Dr. Webster gives 5 lectures per week, in the first and part of the second term, at the Medical College, amounting in the whole to 77 lectures, which the undergraduates do not attend; these lectures requiring for their preparation more time than the more elementary course at Cambridge.

Whole No. of lectures and recitations, 1 hour each,   172 hours.
No. of hours employed in preparation for
   lectures, &c. average $172 \times 6 = 1032$

Total of hours occupied   1204

H.

Department of Botany and Zoology.

This is under the exclusive superintendence of Thomas Nuttall, A. M., Lecturer on Botany and Zoology, and Curator of the Botanical Garden.

Instruction in this department commences in the third term, in Smellie's Philosophy of Natural History, to the Senior Class. From twenty-two to twenty-four recitations are required. These are occasionally accompanied by short lectures, on Zoological subjects; occupying an hour in the morning or forenoon every day.

Voluntary lectures are also given to the Senior and Junior Classes, in the third term, three times a week.

I.

Department of Modern Languages.

This is at present under the superintendence of George Ticknor, A. M., Smith Professor of the French and Spanish Languages and Literature, and Professor of Belles Lettres; assisted by four instructers, *viz.* Francis Sales, Esq., Instructer in French and Spanish; Pietro Bachi, A. M., J. U. D., Instructer in Italian; Charles Follen, J. U. D., Professor of the German Language and Literature; and Francis M. J. Surault, Instructer in French.

The principles which regulate the study of the modern languages are these: 1. No student is compelled to study any one of them. 2. A student, choosing to study any one, is bound to persevere; he is not permitted to quit the study until he has learnt the language. 3. Those, who enter upon the study of any language, are formed into sections, and carried forward according to their proficiency, without reference to the distinction of Classes. 4. The Instructers are paid only for one half their time, and the days of instruction are Mondays, Wednesdays, and Fridays.

The Recitations are held generally during study hours; or A. M. from Study Bell till 12 o'clock, and P. M. from 2 o'clock till prayers; but, to avoid interference with recitations in other branches, some sections have been heard from 12 to 1 o'clock, and some in the evening, during the past year.

Three things should be borne in mind, when considering the state of this department during the academical year of 1830–31.

1. Neither Freshmen nor Seniors attended in it, except as *volunteers*; that is, as Students pursuing the study of some language entirely beyond the regular course. The *regular* Students, therefore, were all either Sophomores or Juniors, who chose some Modern' Language, as a substitute for other prescribed studies.

2. The Graduates attending on the instructions of this department, whose number is considerable, are not noted.

3. During the second term of the academical year, Professor Ticknor delivered a Course of Lectures (three times a week) on the History and Criticism of *French* Literature, to about 60 members of the two upper classes besides Graduates; — the Course being voluntary on his part, and the attendance voluntary on the part of the Students. These also are not noted in the statements below.

First Table.

Number of Undergraduates taught during each term; the languages in which they were instructed; and the proportions of Regular Students and Volunteers.

	French.	Spanish.	Italian.	German.	Portuguese.	Volunteers.	Regular.	Total.
First Term	90	67	34	21		83	129	=212
Second Term	80	34	39	51	8	71	141	=212
Third Term	63	33	72	52	16	97	139	=236

Second Table.

Examinations were held at the end of each Term by the Committee of the Overseers, and there were passed as having learnt,

French 57; Spanish 47; German 20; Italian 8; Portuguese 6.

K.

OMISSIONS AND PUNISHMENTS.
YEAR, 1830-31.
I. Senior Class.

Whole number of the Class	66

Absences from Daily Prayers.

Whole attendance on Daily Prayers required of each
    individual 13 per week, 40 weeks . . 520
Whole do. required of the whole Class in the
    year, 520 × 66 = ... —— 34,320
Whole number of Absences in the first term ending
    December, 1830 1,467
Do. in the second term ending April, 1831, . 1,774
Do. in the third term ending July, 1831, . 1,630
Whole number of absences, excused and unexcused,
    during the year, of this Class, from Daily Prayers, 4,871

The result of this number (4,871) divided by the whole number of the Class (66) shows that the number of absences from Daily Prayers was for the whole year (40 weeks) equivalent to 73 absences, or 24 a term, or about 2 a week for each individual.

In point of fact, four individuals in this Class exceeded, during the first term, 2 absences from this exercise per week, and were *admonished* on that account.

In the second term two were deemed to have exceptionably, and without excuse, exceeded that average, and were *admonished* on that account.

In the third term, two exceptionably, or without excuse, exceeded that average, and were accordingly *admonished*.

Absences from Sabbath Exercises.

Whole number of Sabbath services required of each
    individual for the year 40 × 2 = 80
Whole number required of the whole Class for the
    year 80 × 66 . . . . . —— 5,280
Whole number of absences from Sabbath services the
    first term 50
    Of which were excused 26
    Unexcused 24
Do. do. the second term 62
    Of which were excused . 42
    Unexcused 20

                    Carried over   68   44   112

			Brought over	68	44	112
Do.	do.	the third term	.	.	.	129
	Of which were excused	.	63		
	Unexcused	.	.	.	66

Total of absences, for the year, of } the whole Class .   . —— 241
Of which were excused —— 131
Unexcused . . ——110 services, or half [days' attendance.

It results that the whole number of unexcused absences did not amount for each individual in the whole Class (66) to an absence from one day's service in the year.

In point of fact, there were but two individuals who were absent without excuse more than four (two days' sabbath services) for the year; and they received the appropriate censure.

Absences from Recitations and other Literary Exercises.

Whole number of exercises required of each individual of this Class for the year . . . 791
Do. do. of the whole Class 791 × 66 =   52,206
  Whole number of absences
    The first term   614
    The second term   642
    The third term   750
  Whole number of absences —— 2006

The result of this number (2006) divided by the whole number (66) of the Class shows that the number of absences from these exercises was equivalent to about 30 for the year (40 weeks); or to about 10 a term;—three fourths of an absence a week for each individual.

In point of fact, five individuals of this Class, on account of their number of absences, and general inattention, were subjected to *admonition*.

II. JUNIOR CLASS.

Whole number of the Class 73

Absences from Daily Prayers.

Whole attendance on Daily Prayers required of each individual (13 per week, 40 weeks in the college year) = 520
Do. do. required of the whole Class in the year (520 × 73) = ... - 37,960
Whole number of absences in the first term   1,137
  "   "   "   second "   740
  "   "   "   third   " 1,105
Whole number excused and unexcused —— 2,982

The result of this number (2982), divided by the whole number of the Class (73), shows that the number of absences from daily prayers was, for the whole year (40 weeks), equivalent to 40 absences, or about 12 a term, or one a week for each individual.

In point of fact, no student of the Junior Class exceeded, in the first or second term, an average of two absences from Daily Prayers per week; and two only in the third term, exceeding that average, were deemed subjects of *admonition*.

Absences from Sabbath Exercises.

Whole number of Sabbath services required of each
individual, two a Sabbath, (40 × 2) =   80
Do.   do.   required of the whole Class for the year
(80 × 73) = ...   5,840
Whole number of absences from Sabbath
services the first term   .   .   .   84
   Of which were excused   .   .   .   38
   Unexcused   46
Do.   do.   the second term   .   .   39
   Of which were excused   .   .   .   28
   Unexcused   11
Do.   do.   the third term   .   .   117
   Of which were excused   .   .   .   78
   Unexcused   39
Whole number of absences for the year ——
for the whole Class   .   .   240
   Of which were excused   .   .   .   144 ——
   Unexcused   .   .   .   . 96 services,
[half-days' attendance.

It results, that the whole number of unexcused absences amounted for each individual in the whole Class (73) to an absence of about one (half-day's) attendance for the year.

In point of fact, no individual had more than *one day's* unexcused absence.

Absences from Recitations and other Literary Exercises.

Whole number of exercises for the year required
of each individual of this Class   .   .   916
Do.   do.   required of the whole Class 916 × 73 =   66,868
Whole number of absences the first term   498
   "   "   second   "   294
   "   "   third   "   471
                                          ————
                                          1,263

The result of this number (1263), divided by the whole number (73) of the Class, shows that the number of absences from Daily Prayers was equivalent to about 17 for the year (40 weeks), to about 6 a term, and less than half an absence a week for each individual.

In point of fact, four were deemed subject to *admonition* for excess of absence and general inattention.

III. Sophomore Class.

Whole number of the Class 60

Absences from Daily Prayers.

Whole attendance on Daily Prayers required of each
individual (13 per week, 40 weeks in the College
year) = ... 520
Do. do. required of the whole Class in the year
(520 × 60) = ... 31,200
Whole number of absences in the first term   1,015
"   "   "   second "   998
"   "   "   third "   948
Whole number, excused and unexcused,   ——— . 2,961

The result of this number (2961), divided by the whole number of the Class (60), shows that the number of absences from Daily Prayers was, for the whole year (40 weeks), equivalent to 49 absences, or to 16 a term, or about *one* a week for each individual.

In point of fact, *two* students exceeded an average of *two* absences per week;

In the second term, *three* exceeded that average;

In the third term, *three* exceeded that average; — all of whom were subjected to admonition on that account.

Absences from Sabbath Exercises.

Whole number of Sabbath services required of each
individual for the year (40 × 2) = . 80
Do. do. required of the whole Class for the year
(80 × 60) = ... 4,800
Whole number of absences from Sabbath services the
first term . . . 48
    Of which were excused . . 29
    Unexcused . . . 19
Do. do. the second term   36
    Of which were excused . . 22
    Unexcused . . . 14
Do. do. the third term   102
    Of which were excused . . 89
    Unexcused . . . 13
Whole number of absences for the year ———
for the whole Class . . 186 ———
Whole number excused . 140 ———
Unexcused . . 46 services, or
[half-days' attendance.

It results that the unexcused absences amount, for each individual in the whole Class (60), to a little exceeding half a service in the year.

Three individuals were absent three days each, without excuse, and were subjected to appropriate censure and admonition.

Absences from Recitations and other Literary Exercises.

Whole number of exercises required of each individual 810
Do. do. of the whole Class (810 × 60) = . . 48,600
Whole number of absences the first term . 545
" " the second " . 627
" " the third " . 236
Amount, for the whole year, for the whole Class, —— 1,408

The result of this number (1408), divided by the whole number of the Class (60), shows that the number of absences from these exercises was equivalent to about 23 for the year (40 weeks) — to 8 for each term, — and a little more than a half of a lesson per week for each individual.

In point of fact, *three* individuals so far exceeded the number of absences, deemed, under the circumstances, reasonable, as to be subject to *admonition* on this account.

IV. FRESHMAN CLASS.

Whole number of the Class 50

Absences from Daily Prayers.

Whole attendance on Daily Prayers required of each individual (13 per week, 40 weeks) = . 520
Do. do. required of the whole Class in the year (520 × 50) = ... 26,000
Whole number of absences in the first term 650
" " " second " 772
" " " third " 785
Whole number of absences, excused and unexcused, of this Class, from Daily Prayers, } —— 2,207

The result of this number (2207), divided by the whole number of the Class (50), shows that the number of absences from Daily Prayers was, for the whole year (40 weeks), equivalent to 44, — or to about 14 a term, — and about *one* a week for each individual.

In point of fact, during the first term, *two* individuals of this Class exceeded the number of absences deemed by the Faculty, under the circumstances, excusable.

During the second, one exceeded that number.

During the third term, five exceeded that number; all the eight above mentioned either on that account, or on account of inattention to study or of conduct in other respects exceptionable, were refused matriculation, and their connexion with the College closed.

Absences from Sabbath Exercises.

Whole number of Sabbath services required of each
   individual for the year (two a week, 40×2) =   80
Do.   do.   required of the whole Class for the
   year (80×50) = ... 4,000
Whole number of absences from Sabbath services
   were, the first term . . . 34
      Of which were excused . . 22
      Unexcused 12
Whole number the second term . 81
      Excused 70
      Unexcused 11
Whole number the third term . 114
      Of which were excused . . . 93
      Unexcused 21
Whole number of absences for the year ——
   for the whole Class . . . 229 ——
Whole number excused . . . . . 185 ——
Unexcused . . . . . . 44 services, or
                                  [half-days' attendance.

It results, that the whole number of unexcused absences amounted for each individual in the whole Class (50) to an absence of less han half a day's attendance in the year.

Absences from Recitations and other Literary Exercises.

Whole number required for the year of each individual   719
Do.   do. of the whole Class (719×50) = . .   35,950
Whole number of absences in
          the first term   :   314
          the second term   .   438
          the third term   .   214
Whole number of absences . . . —— 966

The result of this number (966), divided by the whole number of the Class (50), shows that the number of absences from these exercises was equivalent to about 20 for the year (40 weeks), to about 7 a term; and to half *an absence* a week for each individual.

All the punishments for neglect under this and the preceding head were included in those above specified in the statement under the head of Absence from Daily Prayers.

Punishments belonging to Offences of a high class.

Five were separated permanently from the College for one year; one for a breach of the peace, accompanied by a violation of the laws of the College; four for disorderly conduct; three were taken away by their friends at the suggestion of the Faculty, for neglect of their studies.

L.

Divinity School.

This is under the superintendence of

Rev. Henry Ware, D. D., Hollis Professor of Divinity;

Sidney Willard, A. M., Hancock Professor of the Hebrew and other Oriental Languages;

Rev. Henry Ware, Jun., A. M., Professor of Pulpit Eloquence and the Pastoral Care; and

Rev. John G. Palfrey, A. M., Professor of Biblical Literature.

The course of instruction in the Divinity School occupies three years. The School consists of three classes; the Junior, Middle, and Senior. Instruction is given by all the above named Professors in their several branches.

The Hollis Professor of Divinity attends exercises with each of the Classes through the year; with the Junior Class, in the Evidences of Natural and Revealed Religion; with the Middle Class, in Ecclesiastical History; and with the Senior Class in Christian Theology.

The Hancock Professor of Hebrew gives instruction in that language to the Junior Class.

The Professor of Pulpit Eloquence and the Pastoral Care gives instruction in the composition and delivery of sermons, and the duties of the pastoral office, to the Senior and Middle Classes, and in Elocution to the Junior Class.

The Professor of Biblical Literature gives instruction to each of the three Classes during the year.

A religious service, with preaching, in which one of the Senior Class officiates, takes place once a week, and is attended by all the members of the School. Also, once a week there is an exercise in extemporaneous preaching, by the Students of the two higher Classes.

The present number of Students (December, 1831) is 29.

M.

Medical School.

This is under the superintendence of

James Jackson, M. D., Hersey Professor of the Theory and Practice of Physic.

John C. Warren, M. D., Hersey Professor of Anatomy and Surgery.

Walter Channing, M. D., Professor of Obstetrics and Medical Jurisprudence.

Jacob Bigelow, M. D., Professor of Materia Medica.

John W. Webster, M. D., Erving Professor of Chemistry and Mineralogy.

The Medical School is conducted by the abovenamed Professors at the Massachusetts Medical College in Mason street, Boston. The instruction is given by courses of lectures, delivered by each of the Professors; beginning annually on the third Wednesday in October, and continuing thirteen weeks.

The number of lectures given in the respective courses, is as follows:—

Dr. Jackson gives five lectures a week on the Theory and Practice of Medicine, amounting to 65
And two a week on Clinical Medicine . . 26
————
91
Which are reduced by omissions on Christmas and Thanksgiving days . . . 2
———— 89

Dr. Warren gives five lectures a week on Anatomy and Surgery, amounting to . 65
One lecture a week on the Principles of Surgery amounting to 13
One visit in a week, of two hours' length, at the Hospital, accompanied with Surgical Operations, and Clinical Remarks, amounting to . . 13
————
91
Reduced by omissions on Christmas and Thanksgiving days 2
———— 89
Dr. Bigelow gives 37
Dr. Channing gives about . . . 60
Dr. Webster about 65
————

Total number of lectures given by the Medical Faculty annually, in all the branches taught in the School, ... } . 340

The number of students attending Medical Lectures this season (1830 – 31) is ninety-five.

The above School is devoted exclusively to Medical Students, undergraduates not being permitted to attend.

Two courses of instruction in each branch are required to be attended by each student, in order to obtain a medical degree.

The school in general may be considered to be prosperous.

Besides the above lectures in the Medical School, there is given at Cambridge, by Dr. Jackson, to the undergraduates, a course of lectures on Hygiene, or the means of preserving health and prolonging life; consisting of seven lectures, beginning on the first Monday of the third term, at 11 o'clock, A. M., and continued daily except on Saturday.

Also a course of lectures on Anatomy, by Dr. Warren, consisting of twenty-five lectures, beginning in April, and ending in May or June.

N.

LAW SCHOOL.

This is under the superintendence of the Hon. Joseph Story, LL.D., Dane Professor of Law; and John Hooker Ashmun, A. M., Royall Professor of Law.

The course of instruction in the Law School is as follows: —

1. *Lectures*, by the *Dane Professor of Law*, on the Law of Nature and Nations, and on Chancery, Commercial, Civil, and Constitutional Law. Lectures, by the *Royall Professor*, on miscellaneous branches of the Common Law.

2. Reviews and examinations of the students in the Text Books. These are held four days in the week, and the time occupied by each varies from one to two hours for each class. The course of study embraces a selection of the best elementary works in each branch of the Law, and is intended to be completed in three years. The students are referred to a series of leading cases in the English and American Reports, and to a parallel course of reading, in addition to the prescribed course of study.

3. *Moot Courts*, for the arguing of questions of law. These are held every week, by one of the Professors; four of the students, in rotation, appear as counsel. They begin to take their turn at the commencement of the second year. They have extempore disputations and debates on legal and miscellaneous questions, as voluntary exercises.

4. Written dissertations on subjects connected with the course of study are occasionally rendered.

5. The students are instructed in the practice of the courts, in the making of writs, preparation of pleadings, and other legal instruments; and an opportunity is afforded for acquiring the routine of office practice.

Course of Study.

Regular Course.	Parallel Course.
Blackstone's Commentaries.	Sullivan's Lectures.
Woodeson's Lectures.	Hale's History of the Common Law.
Kent's Commentaries.	Hoffman's Legal Outlines.

LAW OF PERSONALTY.

Bacon's Abridgment, selected titles.	Angell on Limitations.
Dane's Abridgment, do. do.	Bingham on Infancy.
Chitty on Contracts.	Collinson on Idiots and Lunatics.
Phillips on Evidence.	Hammond's Nisi Prius.
Stephen on Reading.	Kyd on Awards.
Chitty on Pleading.	Kyd on Corporations.
Saunders's Reports and Notes.	Reeve's Domestic Relations.
Select Cases.	Reeve's History of English Law.
Starkie on Evidence.	Roberts on the Statute of Frauds.
	Roper on Legacies.
	Roper on Husband and Wife.
	Starkie on Slander.
	Toller's Executors.

COMMERCIAL AND MARITIME LAW.

Bacon's Abridgment, "Merchant."	Long on Sales.
Dane's do. "Insurance."	Phillips on Insurance.
Bailey on Bills.	Benecke on Insurance.
Abbott on Shipping.	Livermore on Agency.
Paley on Agency.	Stevens on Average.
Marshall on Insurance.	Azuni's Maritime Law.
Story on Bailments.	
Gow on Partnership.	
Fell on Guarantee.	
Selected Cases from the Reports.	

LAW OF REAL PROPERTY.

Coke on Littleton.	Runnington on Ejectment.
Cruise's Digest — Select titles.	Sanders on Uses and Trusts.
Fearne on Contingent Remainders.	Powell on Mortgages.
Preston on Estates.	Angell on Water Courses.
Dane's Abridgment — Select titles.	Woodfall's Landlord and Tenant.
Stearns on Real Actions.	Sugden's Vendors.
Select Cases.	Jackson on Real Actions.

EQUITY.

Barton's Suit in Equity.	Fonblanque's Equity.
Cooper's Pleadings.	Redesdale's Pleadings.
Jeremy's Equity Jurisdiction.	Beame's Pleas in Equity.
Newland on Chancery Contracts.	Eden on Injunctions.
Select Cases.	Hoffman's Master in Chancery.

CROWN LAW.

East's Crown Law.	
McNally's Evidence.	
Russell on Crimes.	
Select Cases.	

CIVIL LAW.

Gibbon's Roman Empire, Ch. 44.	Pothier on Obligations.
Justinian's Institutes.	Domat's Civil Law — Select Titles.
	Brown's Civil Law.
	Butler's Horæ Juridicæ.

Regular Course.	Parallel Course.
LAW OF NATIONS.	
Martens' Law of Nations.	Ward's Law of Nations.
Rutherforth's Institutes.	Vattel's do.
	Bynkershoek's Law of War.
CONSTITUTIONAL LAW.	
American Constitutions.	The Federalist.
Select Cases in Reports.	Rawle on the Constitution.

The number of students during the past year has been 41. They have been usually divided into two classes according to seniority and advancement. Their attendance upon the exercises has been hitherto wholly voluntary; and has been marked by a punctuality and by a degree of advancement highly satisfactory. The opportunity of pursuing the study of the profession at the School is considered as a privilege, and the students themselves are understood to have been well satisfied with the arrangements.

O.

GENERAL STATEMENT OF ALL PERSONS RESIDENT AT THE UNIVERSITY, EITHER AS GRADUATES OR UNDERGRADUATES.

Graduates.

Theological Students	31	
Students attending Medical Lectures	95	
Law Students	41	
Resident Graduates	1	
		168

Undergraduates.

Seniors	70	
Juniors	55	
Sophomores	50	
Freshmen	60	
Students not candidates for a degree	2	
		237
Total		405

*** The annexed Tables exhibit the time and objects of the successive recitations of every Class in each term of the academic year.

FIRST TERM.

MONDAY.

Classes.	Sections.	After Prayers.	Study Bell.	IX to X.	X to XI.	XI to XII.		IIId. hour before Prayers, P. M.	IId. hour before Prayers, P. M.	Ist. hour before Prayers, P. M.
Seniors.	I. II. III. IV.	Natural Philo- phy } D. Do. } D.	**Modern Languages.**					. . . .	Intellectual } D. Philosophy	Intellectual } D. Philosophy
Juniors.	I. II. III. IV.	Intellectual Phi- losophy } D.	Intellectual } D. Phil phy		**Modern Languages.**				Greek Latin	Greek Latin
Sophomores.	I. II. III. IV.	Greek Latin	Greek Latin	. . . . . .	Theolog. } S. Mathematics Mathematics	Theolog. } S. Mathematics		**Modern Languages.**		
Freshmen.	I. II. III. IV.	Greek Latin	Greek Latin	. . . . . .	Mathematics Mathematics	Mathematics		. . . . . .	Greek Latin	Greek Latin

TUESDAY.

Classes.	Sections.	After Prayers.	Study Bell.	IX to X.	X to XI.	XI to XII.		IIId. hour before Prayers, P. M.	IId. hour before Prayers, P. M.	Ist. hour before Prayers, P. M.
Seniors.	I. II. III. IV.	Natural Phil- ophy } D. Do. } D.			Optics } D.	Optics } D.			Intellectual } D. Philosophy	Intellectual } D. Philosophy
Juniors.	I. II. III. IV.	Intellectual Phi- losophy } D.	Intellectual } D. Phil phy		Theology } D.	Theology } D.			Greek Latin	Greek Latin
Sophomores.	I. II. III. IV.	Greek Latin	Greek Latin		Greek Latin	Greek Latin			Ms ths	Ms M
Freshmen.	I. II. III. IV.	Greek Latin	Greek Latin		Mathematics Mermatics	Mathematics Mth atis			Greek Latin	Greek Latin

a

FIRST TERM CONTINUED.

WEDNESDAY.

Classes.	Sections.	After Prayers.	Study Bell.	IX to X.	X to XI.	XI to XII.	IIId. hour before Prayers, P. M.	IId. hour before Prayers, P. M.	Ist. hour before Prayers, P. M.
Seniors.	I. II. III. IV.	Natural Philosophy } D. Do. } D.	Modern languages.					Intellectual } D. Philosophy }	Intellectual } D. Philosophy }
Juniors.	I. II. III. IV.	Intellectual Philosophy } D.	Intellectual } D. Philosophy }	Modern languages.				Greek Latin	Greek Latin
Sophomores.	I. II. III. IV.	Greek Latin	Greek Latin		Rhet.&Log. } S.	Rhet.&Log. } S.			
Freshmen.	I. II. III. IV.	Greek Latin	Greek Latin		Mathematics Mathematics	Mathematics Mathematics		Greek Latin	Greek Latin

THURSDAY.

Seniors.	I. II. III. IV.	Natural Philosophy } D. Do. } D.			Optics } D.	Optics } D.		Intellectual } D. Philosophy }	Intellectual } D. Philosophy }
Juniors.	I. II. III. IV.	Intellectual Philosophy } D.	Intellectual } D. Philosophy }		Theology } D.	Theology } D.		Greek Latin	Greek Latin
Sophomores.	I. II. III. IV.	Greek Latin	Greek Latin		Greek Latin	Greek Latin		Mathematics Mathematics	Mathematics Mathematics
Fresh	I. II.	Greek Latin	Greek Latin		Mathematics Mathematics	Mathematics		Greek Latin	Greek

FIRST TERM CONTINUED.

Classes.	Sections.	After Prayers.	Study Bell.	IX to X.	X to XI.	XI to XII.	FRIDAY.	III^d. hour before Prayers, P.M.	II^d. hour before Prayers, P.M.	Ist. hour before Prayers, P.M.
Seniors.	I. II. III. IV.	Natural Philosophy }D. Do. }D.	Modern Languages.				· · · · · · · · · · · ·		Forensics every other week. Themes every intermediate week, alternating with the Juniors. To the whole Class.	
Juniors.	I. II. III. IV.	Intellectual Philosophy }D.	Intellectual Philosophy }D.	Modern Languages.			· · · · · · · · · · · ·		Forensics every other week. Themes every intermediate week, alternating with the Seniors. To the whole Class.	
Sophomores.	I. II. III. IV.	Greek Latin	Greek Latin	· · · · · ·	Mathematics Mathematics	Mathematics Mathematics	· · · · · · · · ·		Modern Languages.	
Freshmen.	I. II. III. IV.	Greek Latin	Greek Latin	· · · · · ·	Greek Latin	Greek Latin	· · · · · · · · ·		Mathematics Mathematics	Mathematics Mathematics
							SATURDAY.			
Seniors.	I. II. III. IV.	Natural Philosophy }D. Do. }D.								
Juniors.	I. II. III. IV.	Intellectual Philosophy }D.	Intellectual Philosophy }D.	· · ·	Theology }D.	Theology }D.				
Sophomores.	I. II. III. IV.	Mathematics Mathematics	Mathematics Mathematics	Themes, in Divisions, alternating weekly, so that Divisions reciting at Study Bell do not attend with Themes.		· · ·				
Freshm	I. II. III.	Greek Antiquities Roman Antiquities.	Gr. Antiquities		Gen. History Gen. History	· ·				

SECOND TERM.

Classes.	Sections.	After Prayers.	Study Bell.	IX to X.	X to XI.	XI to XII.		IIId. hour before Prayers, P. M.	IId. hour before Prayers, P. M.	1st. hour before Prayers, P. M.
							MONDAY.			
Seniors.	I. II. III. IV.	Moral & Politi- } D. cal Philosophy }	Mor. & Pol. } D. Philosophy }	Modern Languages.				. . . .	Lectures on Theology to whole Class	. . . .
Juniors.	I. II. III. IV.	Natural Philos- } D. ophy } Do. } D.			Modern Languages.				. Greek . Latin	. Greek . Latin
Sophomores.	I. II. III. IV.	. Greek . Latin	. Greek . Latin		. Rhet. & Log. } S. . .	Rhet. & Log. } S. . .			. Greek . Latin	. Greek . Latin
Freshmen.	I. II. III. IV.	. Greek . Latin	. Greek . Latin		Mathematics Mathematics	Mathematics Mathematics			Mathematics Mathematics	Mathematics Mathematics
							TUESDAY.			
Seniors.	I. II. III. IV.	Moral & Politi- } D. cal Philosophy }	Mor. & Pol. } D. Philosophy }		Lectures on Intellectual Philosophy to whole Class	. . . .			Lectures on Theology to whole Class	. . . .
Juniors.	I. II. III. IV.	Natural Philos- } D. ophy } Do. } D.			Chemistry { D. Do. { D.	Lectures on Rhetoric and Oratory to whole Class			. Greek . Latin	. Greek . Latin
Sophomores.	I. II. III. IV.	. Greek . Latin	. Greek . Latin		. Greek . Latin	. Greek . Latin			Mathematics Mathematics	Mathematics Mathematics
Freshmen.	I. II. III. IV.	. Greek . Latin	. Greek . Latin		Mathematics Mathematics	Mathematics Mathematics			. Greek . Latin	. Greek . Latin

SECOND TERM CONTINUED.

Classes.	Sections.	After Prayers.	Study Bell.	IX to X.	X to XI.	XI to XII.	WEDNESDAY. IIId. hour before Prayers, P. M.	IId. hour before Prayers, P. M.	1st. hour before Prayers, P. M.
Seniors.	I. II. III. IV.	Moral & Politi- cal Philosophy } D.	Mor. & Pol. Philosophy } D.	. . . .	𝔐𝔬𝔡𝔢𝔯𝔫 𝔏𝔞𝔫𝔤𝔲𝔞𝔤𝔢𝔰.	𝔐𝔬𝔡𝔢𝔯𝔫 𝔏𝔞𝔫𝔤𝔲𝔞𝔤𝔢𝔰.	. . . .	Lectures on Theology to whole Class	. . . .
Juniors.	I. II. III. IV.	Natural Philos- ophy Do. } D. } D.	. . .	𝔐𝔬𝔡𝔢𝔯𝔫 𝔏𝔞𝔫𝔤𝔲𝔞𝔤𝔢𝔰.	. Greek . Latin	. Greek . Latin	𝔐𝔬𝔡𝔢𝔯𝔫 𝔏𝔞𝔫𝔤𝔲𝔞𝔤𝔢𝔰.	. Greek . Latin	. Greek . Latin
Sophomores.	I. II. III. IV.	. Greek . Latin	. Greek . Latin	. . .	Rhet. & Log. } S.	Rhet. & Log. } S.	. . .	. Greek . Latin	. Greek . Latin
Freshmen.	I. II. III. IV.	. Greek . Latin	. Greek . Latin	. . .	Mathematics Mathematics	Mathematics Mathematics	. . .	Greek Latin	Greek Latin
						THURSDAY.			
Seniors.	I. II. III. IV.	Moral & Politi- cal Philosophy } D.	Mor. & Pol. Philosophy } D.	. . .	Lectures on Intellectual Philosophy to whole Class	Lectures on Rhetoric and Oratory to whole Class	. . .	. . .	. . .
Juniors.	I. II. III. IV.	Natural Philos- ophy Do. } D. } D.	. . .	. . .	Chemistry } D. Do. } D.	. Greek . Latin	. . .	. Greek . Latin	. Greek . Latin
Sophomores.	I. II. III. IV.	. Greek . Latin	. Greek . Latin	. . .	Mathematics Mathematics	Mathematics Mathematics	. . .	Mathematics Mathematics	Mathematics Mathematics
Freshmen.	I. II. III. IV.	. Greek . Latin	. Greek . Latin,	. . .	Mathematics Mathematics	Mathematics Mathematics	. . .	. Greek . Latin	. Greek . Latin

b

SECOND TERM CONTINUED.

Classes.	Sections.	After Prayers.	Study Bell.	IX to X.	X to XI.	XI to XII.	FRIDAY.	IIId. hour before Prayers, P. M.	IId. hour before Prayers, P. M.	Ist. hour before Prayers, P. M.
Seniors.	I. II. III. IV.	Moral & Politi- cal Philosophy } D.	Mor. & Pol. } D. Philosophy	Modern Languages.			. . . .		Forensics every other week. Themes every intermediate week, alternating with the Juniors. To the whole Class.	
Juniors.	I. II. III. IV.	Natural Philos- ophy } D. Do. } D.		Modern Languages.			. . . .		Forensics every other week. Themes every intermediate week, alternating with the Seniors. To the whole Class.	
Sophomores.	I. II. III. IV.	Greek . Latin Greek . Latin	Greek Latin Greek Latin	. . . .	Mathematics Mathematics Greek Latin	Mathematics Mathematics Greek Latin	. . . .	Modern Languages.		
Freshmen.									Mathematics Mathematics	Mathematics Mathematics

SATURDAY.

Classes.	Sections.	After Prayers.	Study Bell.	IX to X.	X to XI.
Seniors.	I. II. III. IV.	Moral & Politi- cal Philosophy } D.	Mor. & Pol. } D. Philosophy	. . . .	. . . .
Juniors.	I. II. III. IV.	Natural Philos-} D. ophy Do. } D.		. . . .	Chemistry } D. Do. } D.
Sophomores.	I. II. III. IV.	Mathematics Mathematics	Mathematics Mathematics	Themes, in Divisions, alter- nating weekly, so that Divi- sions reciting at Study Bell do not attend with Themes.	
Freshmen.	I. II. III. IV.	Greek Antiquities Roman Antiquities	Gr. Antiquities R. Antiquities	Gen. History } D. Gen. History } D.	

THIRD TERM.

MONDAY.

Classes.	Sections.	After Prayers.	Study Bell.	IX to X.	X to XI.	XI to XII.	IIId. hour before Prayers, P. M.	IId. hour before Prayers, P. M.	1st. hour before Prayers, P. M.
Seniors.	I. II. III. IV.	Moral & Political Philosophy } D.	Mor. & Pol. Philosophy } D.	Philos. of Nat. Hist. } D.	Philos. of Nat. Hist. } D.	. .	. .	Lectures on Mineralogy to whole Class	Lectures on Anatomy to whole Class
Juniors.	I. II. III. IV.	Natural Philosophy } D. Do. } D.	**Modern Languages.**	. .	. .	Experimental Lectures in Natural Philos. to whole Class	. .	Greek . Latin	Greek . Latin
Sophomores.	I. II. III. IV.	Greek . Latin	Greek . Latin	. .	Rhet.&Log. } S.	Rhet.&Log. } S.	**Modern Languages.**	Greek . Latin	Greek . Latin
Freshmen.	I. II. III. IV.	Greek . Latin	Greek . Latin	. .	Mathematics Mathematics	Mathematics Mathematics	. .	. .	. .

TUESDAY.

Classes.	Sections.	After Prayers.	Study Bell.	IX to X.	X to XI.	XI to XII.	IIId. hour before Prayers, P. M.	IId. hour before Prayers, P. M.	1st. hour before Prayers, P. M.
Seniors.	I. II. III. IV.	Moral & Political Philosophy } D.	Mor. & Pol. Philosophy } D.	Philos. of Nat. Hist. } D.	Philos. of Nat. Hist. } D.	. .	. .	Mineralogy, from about the middle of the term, to whole Class	Lectures on Anatomy to whole Class
Juniors.	I. II. III. IV.	Natural Philosophy } D. Do. } D.	. .	. .	Chemistry, to about the middle of the term, to whole Class	Experimental Lectures in Natural Philos. to whole Class	. .	Greek . Latin	Greek . Latin
Sophomores.	I. II. III. IV.	Greek . Latin	Greek . Latin	. .	Greek . Latin	Greek . Latin	. .	Mathematics Mathematics	Mathematics Mathematics
Freshmen.	I. II. III. IV.	Greek . Latin	Greek . Latin	. .	Mathematics Mathematics	Mathematics Mathematics	. .	Greek . Latin	Greek . Latin

THIRD TERM CONTINUED.

WEDNESDAY.

Classes	Sections	After Prayers.	Study Bell.	IX to X	X to XI	XI to XII	¼ hour before Prayers, P.M.	1 hour before Prayers, P.M.	1st hour before Prayers, P.M.
Seniors.	I. II. III. IV.	Moral & Politi- } D. cal Philosphy }	Mor. & Pol. } D. Philosophy }	Philos. of } Nat. Hist. }	Philos. of } D. Nat. Hist. }		. . . .	. . . .	Lectures on Anatomy to whole Class
Juniors.	I. II. III. IV.	Natural Philos- } D. ophy Do. } D.	Modern Languages.			Experimental Lectures in Natural Philos. to whole Class	. . . .	. . . .	. . . .
Sophomores.	I. II. III. IV.	. Greek . Latin	. Greek . Latin	. . . .	Rhet. & Log. } s.	Rhet. & Log. } s.	. . . .	. . . .	. . . .
Freshmen.	I. II. III. IV.	. Greek . Latin	. Greek . Latin	. . . .	Mathematics Mathematics	Mathematics Mathematics	. . . .	. Greek . Latin	. Greek . Latin

THURSDAY.

Classes	Sections	After Prayers.	Study Bell.	IX to X	X to XI	XI to XII	¼ hour before Prayers, P.M.	1 hour before Prayers, P.M.	1st hour before Prayers, P.M.
Seniors.	I. II. III. IV.	Moral & Politi- } D. cal Philosophy }	Mor. & Pol. } D. Philosophy }	Philos. of } Nat. Hist. } D.	Philos. of } D. Nat. Hist. }		. . . .	Mineralogy, from about the middle of the term, to whole Class	Lectures on Anatomy to whole Class
Juniors.	I. II. III. IV.	Natural Philos- } D. ophy Do. } D.	. . . .	. . . .	Chemistry, to about the middle of the term, to whole Class	Experimental Lectures in Natural Philos. to whole Class	. . . .	. . . .	. . . .
Sophomores.	I. II. III. IV.	. Greek . Latin	. Greek . Latin	. . . .	Greek Latin	Greek Latin	. . . .	. Greek . Latin	. Greek . Latin
Freshmen.	I. II. III. IV.	. Greek . Latin	. Greek . Latin	. . . .	Mathematics Mathematics	Mathematics	. . . .	. Greek . Latin	Mathematics Mathematics Greek

THIRD TERM CONTINUED.

Classes.	Sections.	After Prayers.	Study Bell.	IX to X.	X to XI.	XI to XII.	FRIDAY.	IIId. hour before Prayers, P.M.	IId. hour before Prayers, P.M.	Ist. hour before Prayers, P.M.
Seniors.	I. II. III. IV.	Moral & Political Philosophy } D.	Mor. & Pol. Philosophy } D.	Philos. of Nat. Hist.	{ D. Philos. of } D. Nat. Hist.	See note A.	. . .	. . .	Forensics every other week. Themes every intermediate week, alternating with the Juniors. To the whole Class.	
Juniors.	I. II. III. IV.	Natural Philosophy } D. Do. } D.	𝕸𝖔𝖉𝖊𝖗𝖓 𝕷𝖆𝖓𝖌𝖚𝖆𝖌𝖊𝖘.				. . .	. . .	Forensics every other week. Themes every intermediate week, alternating with the Seniors. To the whole Class.	
Sophomores.	I. II. III. IV.	Greek Latin	Greek Latin	. . . . . .	Mathematics Mathematics	Mathematics Mathematics	. . .	. . .	𝕸𝖔𝖉𝖊𝖗𝖓 𝕷𝖆𝖓𝖌𝖚𝖆𝖌𝖊𝖘.	Mathematics Mathematics
Freshmen.	I. II. III. IV.	Greek Latin	Greek Latin	. . .	Greek Latin	Greek Latin	. . .	. . .		Mathematics Mathematics

SATURDAY.

Classes.	Sections.	After Prayers.	Study Bell.	IX to X.	X to XI.					
Seniors.	I. II. III. IV.	Moral & Political Philosophy } D.	Mor. & Pol. Philosophy } D.	Philos. of Nat. Hist.	{ D. Philos. of } D. Nat. Hist.					
Juniors.	I. II. III. IV.	Natural Philosophy } D. Do. } D.			Chemistry, to about the middle of the term, to whole Class					
Sophomores.	I. II. III. IV.	Mathematics Mathematics	Mathematics Mathematics	Themes, in Divisions, alternating weekly, so that Divisions reciting at Study Bell do not attend with Themes.						
Freshmen.	I. II. III. IV.	Greek Antiquities Roman Antiquities	Gr. Antiquities R. Antiquities	. . .	Gen. History } D. Gen. History } D.					

TREASURER'S STATEMENT.

The Treasurer herewith presents his annual statement of the pecuniary concerns of the College.

The account No. I. is a digest of the money transactions, and shows the whole amount of the actual receipts and payments during the College year.

The account No. II. shows the actual income for the general purposes of the College and for the instruction of the Undergraduates. It will be perceived that the expenditure has exceeded the income by the sum $4438·31.

This excess is accounted for,

By an increase in the amount paid for instruction of nearly	$5000
By payments in the settlement of old accounts and other items not belonging to the regular College Expenses, say	2000
By payment within the current year of a part of the expenses of two years, amounting extra to	2500
In addition to the above about	6500
has been expended on the Library, and the relative income has been less about	2000

in consequence of the low rate of interest.

The accounts No. III. show the state of the Commons, Wood, and Class Books, which are for the accommodation of the Students, and are intended to balance, as nearly as possible, without either gain or loss to the College.

The accounts No. IV. show the state of the Law and Divinity Schools.

There is a balance against the Law School of $3485·01, but upwards of 6000 dollars have been expended on the Law Library, which is charged to this account, so that there has been a gain of between two and three thousand dollars, and it is expected that the Law School will gradually pay its debt and leave the Library clear without cost to the College.

The funds of the Divinity School have only recently been placed wholly with the College government. Extensive repairs have been required, and other expenses incurred, which have been paid from the funds held in trust or subscribed for this department. The other accounts, it is believed, present all that is requisite to a full understanding of the College funds and property. The Treasurer begs to state, that the extra payments of the last year, which cannot again occur, were greater in amount than the over expenditure, and that by lessening the appropriation for Books, the expenditure of the coming year may be kept at pleasure within the income, which will probably exceed that of the last year, while some of the ordinary expenses of the College will be diminished.

Which is respectfully submitted.

T. W. WARD, *Treas. Harv. Coll.*

Harvard College, November 17, 1831.

No. I.

ACCOUNT OF CASH RECEIPTS AND DISBURSEMENTS BY THE TREASURER, AND INCOME AND EXPENDITURE THROUGH THE STEWARD'S DEPARTMENT, FOR THE YEAR ENDING AUGUST 31, 1831.

RECEIPTS AND INCOME.

Balance of the Steward's account, August 31, 1830, for term bills not then collected		7,408·31
Balance of Cash in hands of late Treasurer, E. Francis Esq. paid		72·20
INTEREST,— received on Notes and Mortgages	16,221·65	
on Term Bill	1·20	
		16,222·85
DIVIDENDS,— Bank Stock	331·00	
Shares, in Charles River Bridge, West Boston Bridge, and Middlesex Canal	558·00	
		889·00
ANNUITIES,— Charles River Bridge, Warren Bridge, West Boston Bridge, John Nugate's and John Glover's, for 1 year	1,366·64	
First payment of Mr. S. Cabot's bond	500·00	
		1,866·64
RENTS,— of Houses and Lands	4,295·08	
of Pews	7·00	
		4,302·08
INCOME,— Amount charged Undergraduates during the year for Instruction, Room Rent, Care of Rooms, Library and Lecture Rooms, Catalogues and Commencement Dinners, in the Term Bills	21,111·52	
Amount received for advanced standing	780·00	
Do. for Degrees and Diplomas	802·50	
		22,694·02
FOR WOOD,— Amount charged in Term Bills	3,077·40	
Do. received for Wood sold otherwise	146·73	
		3,224·13
FOR REPAIRS,— Amount charged Students in Term Bills for Special Repairs	593·86	
Received otherwise for damage to Rooms	37·75	
Do. for old Materials sold	73·80	
		705·41
FOR COLLEGE FURNITURE,— sold	27·70	
Received of J. Whitney, Contractor for Commons, for use of furniture in his department, for the year, and breakage	378·48	
		406·18
FOR COMMONS,— Amount charged Students, for Board in Commons		8,865·62
FOR TEXT BOOKS,— Amount charged Students for Class Books	2,175·32	
Received of Boston Marine Insurance Company for damage of Books per Lima, wrecked	36·00	
		2,211·32
NOTES AND MORTGAGES,—		
Amount paid off during the year	58,485·76	
Do. received of N. I. Bowditch on account of notes in his hands for collection	50·00	
Do. of annual payments on notes called "Suspended Notes"	370·00	
		58,905·76
Dividend from shares in former United States Bank		220·00
Amount forward		$127,993·52

No. I. Continued.
RECEIPTS AND INCOME.

Amount forward		$127,993·52
To credit of Library,		
Amount of Hilliard and Brown for Catalogues sold	85·05	
Do. of duties on Books paid, refunded	6·28	
		91·33
For sale of College Lands in Sedgwick	348·00	
Less, discount on bills received	88	
		347·12
Hopkins's Beneficiary money of 1830, advanced to A. Brigham, Proctor, refunded		100·00
Of Nahum Hardy, in conformity to his Indenture for the Purchase of the Rogers Farm, Waltham, at expiration of his lease		2,000·00
Dividends on deposits with the Massachusetts Hospital Life Insurance Company to account of		
Reverend Daniel Williams's Legacy	624·00	
Paul Dudley's Legacy	21·33	
		645·33
Exhibition money voted to Gardner in 1830, returned, unpaid,		10·00
Ward N. Boylston's Medical Prizes for 4 years, to August, 1831		400·00
Ward N. Boylston's Prizes for Elocution, for 2 years, to August 31, 1830	180·00	
Amount of bond for principal of these prizes, paid by the Trustees	1,000·00	
With Interest on the same from September 1st, to December 1st, 1830	12·50	
		1,192·50
For account of "Thomas Cary's Legacy" for net sales of Land in Newbury and Charlestown, and rent of same		1,152·89
From the Hopkins Trustees, for the purchase of Books for "Deturs," being 10 per cent of the money given to Divinity Students in 1830, which goes to an account, named "Edward Hopkins's Donation"		70·00
For sale of Stoughton Marsh, Dorchester, to the credit of Exhibition Fund		283·65
For account of the Law School and Library		3,291·50
Do. Theological School		4,210·23
Do. Professorship of Natural History and the Botanic Garden		2,674·36
Do. Count Rumford's Legacy, Income from Trustees in Paris		197·69
For expenses on B. Crombie's notes and mortgages and premium on Fire Insurance, refunded		18·64
		144,678·76
Amount of Checks drawn on Suffolk Bank beyond the deposites, to be discharged by the payment of the Term Bills of the 3d term, which are not payable earlier than the first week in September		4,134·04
		$148,812·80

Note. The Checks of the Treasurer on the Suffolk Bank to the amount of $6,427·25 not being presented at the Bank for payment in August, there appears on the books of the Bank, August 31st, a balance of $2,293·21 due the College Treasurer.

No. I. CONTINUED.

DISBURSEMENTS, &c.

Paid to Account of		
Salaries and Grants	31,433·96	
Expenses	6,003.80	
Profit and Loss	712·81	
Services of Students	673·34	
Repairs	4,914·45	
Library	3,260·18	
Commons, J. Whitney's bills for board of Students	8,865.62	
Count Rumford's Legacy	1,152 84	
Diplomas	62·50	
Text Books	2,374·74	
Interest	57·77	
Wood	964·43	
Income, allowance overcharges on Term Bills	27·00	
Lawyer's fees, suit on B. Crombie's notes, refunded	12·89	
Houses and Lands in Cambridge, paid for building erected by Dr. Hedge, adjoining Sewall House	200·00	
		60,716·33
Paid, Income on Rev. Daniel Williams's Legacy	624·00	
" on Account of Income on Sarah Winslow's Donation	303·79	
" Exhibition money to Undergraduates	1,000·00	
" Boylston Prizes of 1830	10·00	
" Bowdoin Prizes " 1830 $150		
" " " 1831 70		
	220·00	
" for Books for Deturs to account "Edward Hopkins's Donation"	88·88	
" to account of		
Professorship of Natural History	656·86	
Theological School	2,589·96	
Law School	2,026·77	
Ward N. Boylston's Medical Annuity	50·00	
Charges of advertising and selling Stoughton Marsh, Dorchester	20·92	
		7,591·18
Amount loaned on Notes and Mortgages during the year	75,500·00	
Amount of Disbursements		$143,807·51

On the other side of this account the Term Bills for the year are all entered as Income through the Steward's department; but, the term bills for the 3d term not being due until the first week in September, a considerable proportion of them usually remains unpaid on the 31st of August, and, the Steward being charged with their whole amount before collection, a balance always appears against him on the 31st of August in the Treasurer's Books; and accordingly the Balance against the Steward, August 31, 1831, for Term Bills unpaid and not due until September, is   5,005·29

$148,812·80

Harvard College, August 31, 1831.

No. II.

ACCOUNT OF INCOME AND EXPENDITURES FOR THE YEAR ENDING COLLEGE, AND DISTINCT FROM THE LAW AND

EXPENDITURE.

Salaries for the year, viz.
To President Quincy	2,235·00
Professor Ware	1,500·00
Professor Hedge	1,500·00
Professor Popkin	1,500·00
Professor Willard	1,500·00
Professor Farrar	1,500·00
Professor Channing	1,500·00
Professor Webster	1,200·00
Professor Ticknor	600·00
Professor Follen	1,012·78
Professor Warren	500·00
Professor Jackson	500·00
To Mr. Saunders, Steward, to April 6, 1831	716·67
Mr. Sparhawk, Steward, from March 1, 1831	500·00
Professor Norton, from March 1, to March 23, 1830, at $1,040 " 23, to Nov. 30, 1830, at 400 } 340·88 Less, part charged Theological School 40·67	
	300·21
Mr. Sales, Instructer in French and Spanish	1,000·00
Mr. Surault, Instructer in French	500·00
Mr. Bachi, Instructer in Italian	500·00
Mr. Felton, Tutor	645·00
Mr. Sweetser, Tutor 645·00 " for extra services 200·70	
	845·70
Mr. McKean, Tutor	645 00
Dr. Beck, Instructer in Latin	800·00
Dr. Barber, Instructer in Elocution	1,358·36
Mr. Curtis, Proctor	60·00
Mr. Brigham, Proctor	150·00
Mr. Hopkinson, Proctor 150·00 " for Instruction 213·20	
	363·20
Mr. Giles, Proctor 150·00 " for Instruction 199·20	
	349·20
Mr. Hillard, Proctor 150·00 " for Instruction 261·60	
	411.60
Mr. Brown, Proctor, from January 15, 1831	93·75
Mr. Emerson, Instructing in Intellectual Philosophy	43·20
Mr. Nuttall, for Lectures on Zoology for the year	100·00
Mr. Sparhawk, services to late Treasurer	133·55
Dr. Pierce, Secretary of Board of Overseers	60·00
Samuel Newell, as Assistant Steward from January 1, 1831	261·11
For keeping the Records of the Corporation	150·00
Keeping the Treasurer's Books, &c.	300·00
To the late Librarian, Mr. Pierce, 3 quarters	483·75
Amount paid Students for services	673·34
	26,491·42
Amount forward	$26,491 42

(7)

No. II.

AUGUST 31, 1831, APPLICABLE TO THE IMMEDIATE PURPOSES OF THE DIVINITY SCHOOLS AND ACCOUNTS IN TRUST.

INCOME.

Interest on the following Appropriations, Legacies, and Donations, the foundations of various Professorships, for 1 year, to August 31, 1831, and which is applicable to the payment of Salaries, viz.

Appropriations for Professors	575.33
John Alford's Legacy	1,321·36
Nicholas Boylston's Legacy	1,349·40
Thomas Cotton's Donation	7·00
John Cummings's Legacy	83·33
Sarah Derby's Legacy	181·97
Abiel Smith's Legacy	1,101·90
William Erving's Legacy	166·66
Henry Flint's Legacy	15·56
Abner Hersey's Legacy	83·33
Ezekiel Hersey's Legacy	397·60
Jonathan Mason's Legacy	27·50
Esther Sprague's Legacy	87·63
Samuel Eliot's Donation	1,029·50
Samuel Dexter's Legacy	300·21
	6,728·28
First payment of Samuel Cabot Esqr's bond towards Professor Follen's Salary	500·00
	7,228·28

Amount charged in Term Bills,
for Instruction, Room Rent, Care of Rooms, Use of Library, Lecture Rooms, Catalogues and Commencement Dinners — 21,111·52
Received for advanced standing — 780·00

                         21,891·52
Less, overcharges in Term Bills, remitted   27·00
                                       21,864·52

Dividends collected on shares in

Union Bank	25·00
New England Bank	15·00
Massachusetts Bank	60·00
Boston Bank	156·00
State Bank	75·00
Charles River Bridge	74·00
West Boston Bridge	450·00
	855·00

Annuities collected from

Charles River Bridge	333·33
Warren Bridge	333·32
John Nugate's Annuity	16·67
	683·32

                                                      30,631·12

                           Amount forward $30,631·12

No. II.

ACCOUNT OF INCOME AND EXPENDITURE

EXPENDITURE.

Amount forward		$26,491·42
Paid College Sweepers for Care of Rooms, &c.		833·25
Janitor's Wages and Board		287·50
Fuel for the Library, Recitation Rooms, and Care of Fires	480·55	
Candles, Oil, and small Articles of Furniture, &c. for Public Rooms, &c.	93·52	
Acids expended in Exhibitions	16·73	
		590·80
for Trees, Lime, Gravel, and Labor on the College Grounds		411·16
for Table Cloths and Tumblers for Commons Hall		153·83
Advertising		52·83
Printing President's Report	113·56	
" Annual Catalogue	20·00	
" Blanks for Class Reports, Circulars, Notices, Term Bills, &c. &c.	159·85	
		293·41
Watch $36·21 Care of Privies $33·00	69·21	
Sand, Carting sundries and attendance meetings of Students	73·76	
Books for the Chapel and binding	15·50	
Premium on $50,000 Fire Insurance on Library	250·00	
for preparation of Scales of Merit	13·00	
for care of Bath, Engine, and Repairs of Clock	21·50	
for Repairs of Electrical Machine and Philosophical Apparatus	49·12	
		492·09
Charges for the Librarian's Department, for Stationery, Cartridge Paper, &c.	43·12	
Writing and Copying	7·35	
Binding & tying Catalogues of Maps &c.	35·58	
	86·05	
Postages and petty Charges, Steward's Dep't	12·46	
Charges by the President.		
Postages $21·85 Stationery, &c. $19·18 Hired Services $27·50	68·53	
for Copying for the President	15·00	
for arranging and filing official papers for President	5·50	
	20·50	
Charges by the Treasurer.		
Postages, Letters and Pacquets by himself and O. Rich, London	40·35	
for Blank Books and Blanks	10·77	
Expenses of paying Salaries, &c.	16·52	
	67·64	
		255·18
Messengers for notifying Committees, Meetings of Overseers, Corporation, and for Treasurer	77·55	
for Dinners and Horse-keeping for the Committees of the Overseers	256·15	
for Carriage hire for the Committees of the Overseers and for the Corporation on Commencement Day, &c.	93·66	
		427·36
Commencement Expenses, Guard, Attendance, Printing, Music, Dinner, &c.		707·84
Repairs on the College buildings		2,994·81
Banking Commissions, &c. in London	26·23	
Freight of Anatomical figure from Havre, and Books, &c. presented from Liverpool and London, and engraving Library Plate	23·35	
		49·58
Amount forward		$34,041·06

(Continued.)

INCOME.

Amount forward $30,631·12

Received, for College Furniture sold		27·70	
of J. Whitney, Contractor for Commons for use of College Furniture in his Department for the year, and breakage		378·48	
			406·18
Balance of Interest account, deduced as follows, viz.			3,844·40
Whole amount Interest received in Cash	16,222·85		
Amount charged the Law School	169·95		
" transferred from other accounts	1,326·14		
	17,718·94		
" Deduct, Interest paid	57·77		
		17,661·17	
Less, Interest on various Legacies, Donations, &c. towards Salaries, as above	6,728·28		
Interest on Library Fund, to that account	300·00		
Interest due and credited to accounts of Professorship of Natural History, Theological School, Exhibitions, Accumulating Funds, and other accounts in trust, particulars under their separate heads	6,788·49		
		13,816·77	
Balance		3,844·40	

Received from the "Wood Account" towards Rent of Wharf, Wood-yard, and Interest on money furnished — — — 288·33

Amount charged Students in the Term Bills for "Special Repairs," arising from wanton damage to the Rooms, College buildings, &c. and is assessed as a general charge only when the individuals, to whom it properly belongs, are unknown	593·86	
Received for damage to Rooms	37·75	
" for old materials sold	73·80	
		705·41

Amount forward $35,875·44

No. II.

ACCOUNT OF INCOME AND EXPENDITURE
EXPENDITURE.

Amount forward			$34,041·06
Paid for printing Diplomas and filling up		50·00	
Repairs on Houses in Cambridge	683·87		
on Webb Estate, Boston	12·45		
		696·32	
			746·32

Paid to account of the Library.
Ebenezer Francis' Bills for amount of Invoices of Books,

Per Liverpool	440·01	
Hudson, London }		
Mercator, Leghorn } -	1,074·28	
Eliza, Hamburgh }		
Lima, Hamburgh } - -	61·53	
Invincible, Malaga }		
Clematis, Havre, in Feb. 1830	838·68	
Freight bills and Wharfage - -	51·86	
Premium on Insurance - -	52·20	
Bills for Books and Reviews, not imported	250·69	
Bill for binding folios, &c. - -	52·32	
folding and tying Catalogues	34·12	
Printing 750 copies of Catalogue of Maps and Charts - - -	398·21	
Duties on Books per Mercator, at New York, afterwards refunded - -	6·28	
		3,260·18
by Baring, Brothers, & Co. London, amount of Invoices by O. Rich, per		
Hudson, from London - -	1,858·77	
Roscius " - -	218·40	
Coliseum, from Havre }		
Clematis " } - -	705·90	
Swan, from London }		
Virginia " - - -	238·89	
Amount paid O. Rich for Magazines, Reviews, &c. - - -	135·21	
		3,157·17
Amount transferred from Account of Text Books, to which the sums were wrongly charged in 1829.		
for 2 volumes of Ornithology - -	25·00	
Expenses, Copying, twice, orders for Books sent to London -	16·42	
		41·42

Amount to the Library - - - -		6,458·77
Paid sundry sums not strictly within the Expenses of any one year, as follows; viz.		
E. W. Metcalf, for Printing Triennial Catalogue	420·15	
John Prince's bill for a Solar Microscope, in June, 1830 - - - - - -	97·50	
Dr. Ware's bill for extra services, in full therefor	321·07	
W. & S. Jones, London, through Baring, Brothers, & Co. in full of a balance of their account for Philosophical Instruments, from 1815–1830	393·00	
Cost of a Silver Urn presented to the late Treasurer by the Corporation for his valuable services - -	318·16	
Freight and duties on same -	42·50	
	360·66	
Premium for insuring $20,000 on an exposed Mortgage - - - - - - -	20·00	

| Amounts forward | $1,612·38 | $41,246·15 |

No. II.
(CONTINUED.)

INCOME.

		Amount forward		$35,875·44
Received for Degrees and Diplomas				802·50
" Rents, of Houses and Lands in Cambridge		2,434·68		
of Printing Office		242·30		
of the Webb Estate, Boston		1,228·10		
of the Rogers Farm, Waltham		250·00		
of Ward's Island		60·00		
of Coggan's Marsh, Chelsea		70·00		
of Pews		7·00		4,292·08

Received to the credit of the Library.
Amount of an Invoice of Text Books, per "Shamrock," charged last year to this account	120·63	
of Hilliard and Brown, for sale of Library Catalogues	85·05	
of one year's Income to Aug. 31, 1831, on $6000, Library Fund	300·00	
of duties paid on Books, per "Mercator," refunded	6·28	511·96

Amount forward $41,481·98

ACCOUNT OF INCOME AND EXPENDITURE

EXPENDITURE.

Amount forward			$41,246·15
Paid sundry Amounts not strictly within the Expenses of any one year (Continued) Amount forward		1,612·38	
Subscription, for improving Cambridge Common	500·00		
" for sinking a Cistern in Market Square, Cambridge	75·00		
		575·00	
Loss sustained on Text Books, bought and furnished to Students, to January 1, 1831, excluding all charges for care and distribution of same		22·19	
N. I. Bowditch, for examining Land Titles		30·22	
F. Furber, for a survey and plan of the College grounds		33·00	
Loss on Samuel Norwood's note, settled by compromise		28·51	
			2,301·30

Paid the following sums, which belong to the Expenses of the previous College year, 1829–1830, viz.

Repairs, prior to August 31, 1830, on College Buildings and Kitchen	1,166·00		
Do. Dwelling Houses	51·90		
		1,217·90	
Sweepers' bills, prior to August 31, 1830		340·12	
Trees, Gravel, and Labor on College Grounds		201·92	
Advertising	48·61		
Postages by the President	5·44		
Printing President's Report, on the plan of Studies	60·67		
		114·72	
Printing for Commencement of 1830	42·50		
Services for do.	33·00		
		75·50	
Oil, Candles, small articles of Furniture, Smoke Jack, Pump Repairs	42·84		
Janitor's Wages and Board to Aug. 31st	11·51		
Chorister and Care of Clock to Aug. 31, 1830	60·00		
Filling out Diplomas	12·50		
Repairing the "President's Chair"	9·50		
Stationery, Blank Books, and Printing Term Bills	16·75		
		153·10	
Corporation and Committees of Overseers Carriage Hire	41·66		
Committees of Overseers, Horse Expenses, &c.	11·18		
		52·84	
		2,156·10	

Paid Salaries, &c. to Expenses of 1829–1830

Dr. Barber, for Instruction in Elocution to August 31, 1830	100·00		
Mr. Nuttall for Lectures on Zoology to August 31, 1830	100·00		
Mr. Brigham, as Proctor, to Aug. 31, 1830	21·82		
Keeping Corporation Records, from April 1st to August 31, 1830	62·50		
		284·32	

Amount to Expenses of 1829–1830			2,440·42
Amount of Carriage hire for Committees of Overseers, in 1828–1829, brought from Account for Text Books, to which account, when paid, it was erroneously charged			66·50
		Dollars	46,054·37

Receipts belonging to the previous year, 1829–1830.
  Dividend on Shares in Charles River Bridge of
    July, 1830 - - - - -   26·00
  " on Share in Middlesex Canal in January, 1830 - - - - -   8·00
  Amount of Hopkins's Beneficiary money advanced to A. Brigham, Proctor, 1830, refunded - - - -   100·00
                 134·00
                 $41,615·98

Balance, difference between Income and Expenditure -   4,438·39
             Dollars   46,054.37

No. III.

SPECIAL ACCOUNTS FOR THE ACCOMMODATION

Dr. - - - - - - - - - - COM-

For paid J. Whitney, Contractor for Commons for Board	-	8,865·62
		$8,865·62

Dr. - - - - - - - - WOOD

For balance of this account, August 31, 1830 - - -		3,100·12
paid for Sawing, Splitting, Piling, Carting, during the year - - - - - -	826·82	
paid for bark and coal - - - -	129·27	
amount of overcharges in Term Bills deducted	8·34	
		964·43
charged towards Rent of Wharf and Yard and Interest of money used - - - in part - - -		288·33
		$4,352·88

Dr. - - - - - - - - TEXT OR

For balance of this Account, August 31, 1830 - - -		3,816·42
cost of Books purchased in the United States	1,574·58	
" " imported, in German, French, and Spanish Languages - - -	766·08	
General Average and Expenses drying &c. of Books per Lima - - - -	29·89	
cost of Books per Shamrock, in June 1830, brought from account against Library, to which it was then charged - - -	120·63	
abatements on charges in Term Bills - -	4·19	
		2,495·37
		$6,311·79

No. IV.

Dr. - - - - - - - - LAW SCHOOL

For balance, debt against this account August 31, 1830		2,152·44	
of Interest due to Aug. 31, 1831, at 5 per cent.		169·95	
paid during the year, for Books, bought in U. S.	1,900·94		
Invoice of Books per Coliseum from Havre, by Baring, Brothers, & Co. - - - -	176·28		
Hilliard & Brown for Law Books, May 1830, transferred from account of Text Books, to which it was charged - - -	535·75		
		712·03	
			2,612·97
Wood from College Yard $112·50. Wood and Coal, otherwise $31·25 - - - -		143·75	
paid Fire Insurance on $4000 on Library, $32 other Insurance $2·33 - - - -		34·33	
Book Case and covering Books -		45·00	
Printing $5, Advertising $7·25, cleaning $3 - - - - -		15·25	
		60·25	
			238·33
paid Salaries, to Professor Ashmun - -	1,500·00		
to Judge Story - - -	1,000·00		
		2,500·00	
			$7,673·69

No. III.

AND WANTS OF THE STUDENTS

MONS			Cr.
By amount charged Students in the Term Bills for board		-	8,865·62
			$8,865·62

			Cr.
By amount charged Students for Wood, in Term Bills	3,077·40		
received for wood sold otherwise - -	146·73		
			3,224·13
consumed in Lecture Rooms, Steward's and Assistant Steward's Rooms - -	266·25		
delivered the Law School - - -	112·50		
			378·75
By Wood on hand, balance August 31, 1831, 125 Cords,	say		750·00
			$4,352·88

CLASS BOOKS			Cr.
By amount charged Students in Term Bills for Books	2,175·32		
loss on Books per Lima of Boston Marine Ins. Co.	36·00		
the following amounts formerly charged to this account, now transferred, viz.			
Law Books, May 1830 - - 535·75			
Coach hire in 1828–1829 - 66·50			
2 Vols. Ornithology, in 1829 - 25·00			
Copying orders for Books for Library 16·42			
	643·67		
By loss sustained on this account to January 1, 1831, (vide account No. II.) - - - -	22·19		
			2,877·18
Balance, value of Books on hand August 31, 1831 - -			3,434·61
			$6,311·79

No. IV.

AND LIBRARY - - - - - - - Cr.

By received amount of Term Bills, for			
Instruction, &c.	3,233·00		
Books sold	52·50		
	3,285·50		
do. for use of Books during vacation -	6·00		
		3,291·50	
Income for the year on Isaac Royall's Legacy -	397·18		
Nathan Dane's Donation	500·00		
		897·18	

Balance debt against this account August 31, 1831	-	-	3,485·01
			$7,673·69

No. IV.

Dr. - - - - - - THEOLOGICAL INSTITUTION

To paid Salaries, to Professor Norton, due him to Dec. 6, 1830	340·88		
Less, paid by Income of the Dexter Fund	300·21		
		40·67	
to Professor Palfrey, from Feb. 3, 1831		1,138·89	
			1,179·56
beneficiary money to Students			530·00
Repairs, Divinity Hall and Janitor House		1,145·09	
for Furniture and Repairs, $33·06, Work on Grounds, Gravel, &c. $31·25		64·31	
Books and Binding $24·25, Copying, Advertisements, &c. $34·12		58·37	
Janitor's Bills for Wages, care of Rooms, and extra Work		618·83	
for Oil, Wicks, &c. $34·27. Wood Expenses, $14·59		48·86	
Expenses of Public Ceremonies at the close of the year		54·50	
			1,989·96
Balance, August 31, 1831			15,202·60
			$18,902·12

NOTE. About $1500 has been appropriated for the purchase of Books, and will make a charge against the above balance.

Dr. - - - - SUBSCRIPTION FUND FOR PROFESSORSHIP

To paid Professor H. Ware Jr.'s Salary for the year	1,500·00
Balance August 31, 1831	8,866·16
	$10,366·16

NOTE. This fund was subscribed for the payment of the Salary of the Professor for ten years and is gradually decreasing.

Dr. - - - - - - PROFESSORSHIP OF

To paid sundry Bills, approved by the Committee viz.		
Jonathan Gary	17·00	
Jacob H. Bates	20·78	
Joseph Holmes	106·08	
Levi Farwell	13·00	
		156·86
the Curator's Salary for one year to July 1, 1831		500·00
Balance, due to this Professorship August 31, 1831		11,456·64

$12,113·50

No. IV.

AND SCHOOL AND DIVINITY HALL - - - - - Cr.

Balance of this account, August 31, 1830		14,003·56
Received of George Bond, Treasurer	1,083·36	
from Hopkins* Trustees, beneficiary money of 1830 and interest	620·00	
in Term Bills for Rent and Care of Rooms, Instruction, Wood, of Divinity Students, and Rent &c. of Law Students	1,798·19	
on old accounts for Wood and Rent	98·73	
Exhibition money of George Bond, Treasurer	300·00	
Rent of Janitor House	140·01	
Interest to August 31, 1831	758·33	
Subscription of William Sturgis Esq.	100·00	
		4,898·56

$18,902·12

* The Hopkins Fund for assisting Divinity Students is in the hands of Trustees, and does not appear in the Books of the College.

OF PULPIT ELOQUENCE AND PASTORAL CARE - - - Cr.

Balance, value of this fund August 31, 1830	9,779·40
Interest to August 31, 1831	586·76
	$10,366·16

NATURAL HISTORY - - - - - - - Cr.

By balance due this account August 31, 1830		1,524·51
dividends on Bank Stock, October, 1830	257·50	
Bank stocks taken at par value.		
10 shares Union Bank	1,000·00	
5 " New England Bank	500·00	
12 " Massachusetts "	3,000·00	
50 " State Bank	3,000·00	
	7,500·00	
received of J. Heard Jr. Esq. for this account	1,888·13	
	341·23	
	2,229·36	
15 months' Rent of Mrs. Coffin	187·50	
balance of Interest to August 31, 1831	414·63	
		10,588·99
		$12,113·50

NOTE. This Department has lately been placed more immediately under the College Government.

c

No. IV.

Dr. - - - - - - THEOLOGICAL INSTITUTION

To paid Salaries, to Professor Norton, due him to Dec. 6, 1830	340·88		
Less, paid by Income of the Dexter Fund	300·21		
		40·67	
to Professor Palfrey, from Feb. 3, 1831		1,138·89	
			1,179·56
beneficiary money to Students			530·00
Repairs, Divinity Hall and Janitor House		1,145·09	
for Furniture and Repairs, $33·06, Work on Grounds, Gravel, &c. $31·25		64·31	
Books and Binding $24·25, Copying, Advertisements, &c. $34·12		58·37	
Janitor's Bills for Wages, care of Rooms, and extra Work		618·83	
for Oil, Wicks, &c. $34·27. Wood Expenses, $14·59		48·86	
Expenses of Public Ceremonies at the close of the year		54·50	
			1,989·96
Balance, August 31, 1831			15,202·60
			$18,902·12

NOTE. About $1500 has been appropriated for the purchase of Books, and will make a charge against the above balance.

Dr. - - - SUBSCRIPTION FUND FOR PROFESSORS[?]

To paid Professor H. Ware Jr.'s Salary for the year - - 1,5[?]
Balance August 31, 1831 - - - - - - - 8,[?]
                                                        $1[?]

NOTE. This fund was subscribed for the payment of [?] ary of the Professor for ten years and is gradually decr[?]

Dr. - - - - - - -

To paid sundry Bills, approved by the Committ[?]
          Jonathan Gary
          Jacob H. Bates
          Joseph Holmes
          Levi Farwell

    the Curator's Salary for one ye[?]

Balance, due to this Professorship

No. IV.

AND SCHOOL AND DIVINITY HALL - - - - - Cr.

Balance of this account, August 31, 1830 - -		14,003·56
Received of George Bond, Treasurer - - -	1,083·36	
from Hopkins* Trustees, beneficiary money of 1830 and interest - - -	620·00	
in Term Bills for Rent and Care of Rooms, Instruction, Wood, of Divinity Students, and Rent &c. of Law Students -	1,798·19	
on old accounts for Wood and Rent - -	98·73	
Exhibition money of George Bond, Treasurer	300·00	
Rent of Janitor House - - - -	140·01	
Interest to August 31, 1831 - - - -	758·33	
Subscription of William Sturgis Esq. - - -	100·00	
		4,898·56

$18,902·12

* The Hopkins Fund for assisting Divinity Students is in the hands of Trustees, and does not appear in the Books of the College.

OF PULPIT ELOQUENCE AND PASTORAL CARE - - - Cr.

Balance, value of this fund August 31, 1830 - - -		9,779·40
Interest to August 31, 1831 - - - - -		586·76
		$10,366·16

N ... RAL - - - - - - - - Cr.

By balance ... unt August 31, 1830 - - -			1,524·51
divide ... tock, October, 1830 - -		257·50	
Bank ... t par value.			
... h Bank - -	1,000·00		
... England Bank -	500·00		
... sachusetts " -	3,000·00		
... te Bank - - -	3,000·00		
		7,500·00	
... eard Jr. Esq. for this account	1,888·13		
	341·23		
		2,229·36	
... ent of Mrs. Coffin - - -		187·50	
... nterest to August 31, 1831 - -		414·63	
			10,588·99
			$12,113·50

This Department has lately been placed more imme- ... er the College Government.

No. IV.

Dr. - - - - - - - Count Rumford's

For paid Daniel Treadwell, for lectures on the Useful Arts prior to August 31, 1830, and against the balance then due - -	152·00	
Dr. Bigelow for a course of Lectures for the year, to August 31, 1831 - -	1,152·84	
		1,304·84
balance due this Legacy August 31, 1831 - - -		23,064·99
		$24,369·83

The following Accounts in connexion with the Foregoing of the College for the year, as

ACCUMULATING FUNDS—

Dr. - - - - - - - Ward N. Boylston's

Balance August 31, 1831 - - - - - - - 5,262·10

$5,262·10

Dr. - - - - - - - - Panorama

Balance, Deposite in Massachusetts Hospital Life Insurance Company, January 1, 1831	778·01	
with the College Funds - - -	130·67	
		908·68

$908·68

Dr. - - - - - - - - Fund for

Balance, August 31, 1831		
West Boston Bridge Annuity, called	11,111·11	
Amount with the College Funds	15,467·03	
		26,578·14

$26,578·14

No. IV.

LEGACY - - - - - - - - - Cr.

By balance thereof, August 31, 1830 - - - - 23,216·99
   Income from Trustees on a part in their hands - 197·69
   balance of Interest Account to August 31, 1830   955·15
                                                  1,152·84

$24,369·83

WILL EXHIBIT THE HISTORY AND RESULTS OF THE FISCAL CONCERNS ENTERED IN THE TREASURER'S BOOKS.

INCOME AT PRESENT ADDED TO PRINCIPAL.

FUND FOR MUSEUM - - - - - - - - Cr.

By balance hereof August 31, 1830 - - - - 4,985·34
   1 year's Interest on same - - - - - 249·26
   1 year's Interest on W. N. Boylston's Donation
     for Books - - - - - - - 27·50
                                               276·76

$5,262·10

OF ATHENS - - - - - - - - Cr.

By balance of this fund August 31, 1828.
   Deposite with Mass. Hospital Life Ins. Co. - 639·33
   Cash on hand - - - - - 113·63
                                            752·96

accumulations of Interest on deposite with the Hospital Life Insurance Company, added annually to principal, to January 1, 1831, viz.
Principal Jan. 1, 1827 $639·33
          1828 672·28 Int. added 32·95
          1829 707·03 do.   34·75
          1830 742·38 do.   35·35
          1831 778·01 do.   35·63
                                138·68
3 years' Interest on $113·63, to August 31, 1831   17·04
                                             155·72

$908·68

PERMANENT TUTORS - - - - - - Cr.

By balance this Fund, August 31, 1830 - - - 25,206·70
   Annuity West Boston Bridge - - - - 666·66
   Interest for the year, to August 31, 1831 - 704·78
                                                1,371·44

$26,578·14

ACCUMULATING FUNDS (Continued)

Dr. - - - - - - Thomas Cary's Legacy,
Balance, due this Fund, Aug. 31, 1831 - - - - 2,274·42

$2,274·42

Dr. - - - - - - Samuel Parkman's Dona-
Balance, due this Fund, Aug. 31, 1831 - - - - 3,517·75

$3,517·75

Dr. - - - - - George Partridge's Donation,
Balance, due this Fund, Aug. 31, 1831 - - - - - 2,268·94

$2,268·94

ACCOUNTS OF FUNDS IN TRUST FOR VARIOUS PURPOSES, THE INCOME

Dr. - - - - - "Exhibitions," (A Fund for
For amount of Exhibition money voted and paid to
  Freshmen - - - - - - 185·00
  Sophomores - - - - - 310·00
  Juniors - - - - - - 280·00
  Seniors, including Senior fund - - 225·00
               1,000·00
Balance, Aug. 31, 1831. { Principal 17,020·10
         { Income   210·23 17,230·33

$18,230·33

Note. There is also belonging to the Exhibition Fund, the receipts from "William Pennoyer's Annuity in England," arising from the Rent of Christ's Hospital, after deducting a certain amount for the Governors thereof. It is of uncertain receipt, and no Income has been received this year.

Dr. - - - - - Mary Saltonstall's Legacy, (A Fund
Balance, Aug. 31, 1831 { Principal 2,600·00
       { Income 130·00
            2,730·00

Note. The Income of this fund is paid to two such students as the Board of Overseers direct. This year it has not been appropriated.

$2,730·00

INCOME AT PRESENT ADDED TO PRINCIPAL.

(A THEOLOGICAL FUND) - - - - - - Cr.

By balance of this fund, August 31, 1830 - - - 954·02
   received one year's Rent of Land in Newbury   25·00
   net sales of Land in Newbury, less $5, drawing Deeds 799·10
   sales of balance of Lots of Land in Charlestown, one
     moiety - - - - - - - - - 328·79
" amount transferred from the account of these Lots of
   Land, being balance of a former sale, over the esti-
   mated value by the College - - - - 75·00
Interest accruing on this account to Aug. 31, 1831,
   at 5 per cent - - - - - - - - 92·51   1,320·40
                                                                  $2,274·42

TION, (A THEOLOGICAL FUND) - - - - - Cr.

By balance of this fund, Aug. 31, 1830 - - - - 3,350·24
   Interest to August 31, 1831 - - - - - 167·51
                                                                  $3,517·75

(A THEOLOGICAL FUND) - - - - - - Cr.
By balance of this fund, August 31, 1830 - - - 2,160·90
   Interest to August 31, 1831 - - - - - 106·04
                                                                  $2,268·94

OF WHICH IS NOT APPLICABLE TO THE EXPENSES OF THE COLLEGE.

ASSISTING POOR SCHOLARS) - - - - - Cr.

By balance of this Fund, { Capital, various sums
   Aug. 31, 1830   consolidated - 16,757·37
                      { Income, unappropriated, 257·82
                                                   17,015·19
Interest on the principal to Aug. 31, 1831 - - 855·75
John Glover's Annuity, belonging hereto - - 16·66
1 year's Rent, Stoughton Marsh, Dorchester - - 10·00
1 year's Interest on Fund called " Seniors' Exhibition" 60·00
                                                       942·41
Exhibition money voted to Gardner in 1830, returned - 10·00
net Sales of Stoughton Marsh, Dorchester - - 262·73
                                                     $18,230·33

FOR ASSISTING POOR SCHOLARS) - - - - Cr.
By Principal of this fund - - - - - 2,600·00
   Interest for one year, to August 31, 1831 - - - 130·00
                                                              $2,730·00

ACCOUNTS OF FUNDS IN TRUST FOR VARIOUS PURPOSES, THE

Dr. - - - - - - JOANNA ALFORD'S LEGACY,
Balance, August 31, 1831 - - Principal 500·00
          Income 25·00
NOTE. The Income of this fund is appropriated by
the Board of Overseers. No vote has passed the $525·00
present year.

Dr. - - - - - - JAMES BOWDOIN'S LEGACY,
For paid Prizes - - - - - of 1830, 150·00
         1831, 70·00
            220·00
Balance, August 31, 1831 - - - - - - 4,384·39
           $4,604·39

Dr. - - - - - WARD N. BOYLSTON, PRIZES
To balance against this account, August 31, 1830, prizes paid, 155·00
" paid prizes awarded in 1830 - - - - - 10·00
Balance, August 31, 1831 - - Principal 1000·00
        Income, 65·00
          1,065·00
NOTE. The declamations for the prizes of 1831
take place the first day of September, and cannot $1,230·00
be brought into this year's account.

Dr. - PAUL DUDLEY'S LEGACY, (A FUND FOR THE DUDLEIAN
NOTE. The Income for the present year is payable
to Dr. Wayland when called for. The balance
is - - - - - - Principal, 444·44
       Income, 21·33
Dr. - - - - THOMAS HOLLIS'S APPROPRIATION
To carried to the Treasurer's credit - - - 26·00
Balance, August 31, 1831 - - - - - 520·00
          $546·00

Dr. - - - - - - WARD N. BOYLSTON'S
Balance against this account, August 31, 1830, was - - 100·00
Paid for a gold Medal for Dr. Caldwell - - - - - 50·00
Balance, August 31, 1831 - - - - - - - 250·00
          $400·00

Dr. - - - - - EDWARD HOPKINS'S DONATION
Paid for Books for Deturs, by the President's order - - 88·88
Balance, August 31, 1831 - - - - - - 294·49
          $383·37

Dr. - - - SARAH WINSLOW'S DONATION, INCOME
For 2½ per cent. Commissions on interest to the College Treas'r 5·70
Paid during the year.
  Rev. Nath'l Lawrence, minister - - - 133·33
  J. D. Nichols, Schoolmaster, 7th June, 1830, to
   6th Jan'y, 1831 - - - - - 77·77
  C. H. Allen, do. 1st July to Aug. 21, 1829 - 19·00
  Ch's Warren, do. 1st Jan'y to April 1, 1830 - 33·33
  C. B. Kittredge, do. 12th Sept. to Nov. 27, 1828 27·77
  Ch's Fiske, do. 1st May, to June 5, 1829 - 12·59
         303·79
Balance, August, 31, 1831. { Principal 4,558·34
      { Income, 211.21 4,769·55
          $5,079·04

INCOME NOT APPLICABLE TO THE EXPENSES OF THE COLLEGE, (Continued.)

(A FUND FOR POOR STUDENTS.) - - - - - Cr.
By principal, August, 31, 1830 - - - - - 500·00
" Interest for 1 year to August 31, 1831 - - - 25·00
                                                                                                                                                                                             $525·00

FOR PRIZES FOR DISSERTATIONS - - - - - Cr.
Balance, August 31, 1830 - - - - - - - 4,392·28
Interest to August 31, 1831 - - - - - - - 212·11
                                                            $4,604·39

FOR ELOCUTION - - - - - - - - - Cr.
By received of his Executors in November 1830, the
   prizes for the year 1828, 1829, 1830 - - - - 180·00
" the principal of this fund paid Dec. 1, 1830 - 1000·00
" received the Interest on same towards prizes of
   1831, from September 1, 3 months - - - 12·50
                                                       1,012·50
" Interest on $1000, from Dec. 1, 1830, to Aug. 31, 1831, - 37·50
                                                            $1,230·00

LECTURE,) (Principal $444.44 on deposite with Life Ins. Co.) Cr.
By one year's Income of Massachusetts Hospital Life Ins. Co.
   to January 1, 1831 - - - - - - - - 21·33

FOR THE TREASURER - - - - - - - Cr.
Balance, August 31, 1830 - - - - - - - 520·00
By Interest one year, to August 31, 1831 - - - - 26·00
                                                            $546·00

MEDICAL ANNUITY - - - - - - - - Cr.
By received of his Trustees in Nov. 1830, the Annuity
        for 1828, 1829, 1830 - - - - 300·00
  "   "   the Annuity for 1831 - - - 100·00
                                             400·00
                                                    $400·00

(BOOKS FOR DETURS) - - - - - - - Cr.
Balance of this fund August 31, 1830 - - - - 300·92
Interest to August 31, 1831 - - - - 12·45
Received from Hopkins Trustees, 10 per cent. of $700,
   beneficiary money voted in 1830 - - - 70·00   82·45
                                                          383·37

TO MINISTER AND SCHOOLMASTER, TYNGSBORO', &c. - Cr.
Balance, August 31, 1830 - - Principal, 4,558·34
                                 Income, unpaid 292·78
                                                       4,851·12
Interest on principal for one year, to August 31, 1831
   5 per cent. - - - - - - - - - 227·92
                                                       $5,079·04

NOTE. Arrears of payments for several years appear on the other side.

ACCOUNTS OF FUNDS IN TRUST FOR VARIOUS PURPOSES, THE

Dr. - - Rev. DANIEL WILLIAMS'S LEGACY, INCOME PAID
To paid Rev. Phineas Fish, - - - - 416·00
" " Rev. Frederick Baylies, - - - - 208·00
                                                        ─────
                                                        $624·00

OTHER ACCOUNTS,
Dr. - - - - - - - - NOTES,
To balance, August 31, 1830 - - - - 282,165·62
" Amount loaned on Notes and Mortgages, during the year - 75,500·00
" do. loan, to Baptist Church, transferred from that account - 5,939·91
                                                        ─────────
                                                        $363,605·53

There is also an account of Notes, called "Suspended Notes," the principal of which, payable in nine
annual instalments, was August 31st, 1830 - - 3,330·00
Instalments paid in 1831   370·00

        Balance thereof, August 31, 1831 $2,960·00
NOTE. These suspended notes were received, less
the Interest at 6 per cent. and the difference between their cost and par is credited the Interest
account the present year - - - - $1,051·58
The Interest account is also credited by a transfer of
Interest from the Loan to the Baptist church, of - 274·56

Making a transfer to Interest, as stated in No. 2. $1,326·14

Dr. - - - - - - BARING, BROTHERS, & Co.
For cost of £1000 remitted them, - - - - - 4,722·22

                                                        $4,722·22

Dr. - - - - - - - - STOCK.
To decreased value on 2 shares in Charles River Bridge,
    valued in February, 1827, at $4,180, - - 2,180·80
" the following items heretofore entered to the credit
    of stock, but which being specially appropriated are
    now transferred, viz.
Value of Land in Newbury, belonging to Thomas
    Cary's Legacy, as entered - - - - 1,000·00
    do. Stoughton Marsh, belonging to Exhibitions - 350·00
                                                        ─────
                                                        1,350·00
" value of Pew in Waltham Church, included in the
    value of Rogers Farm, Waltham - - - - 150·00
" disbursements more than receipts, per account No. 2 - - 4,438·39
Balance, August, 1831 - - - - - - 153,518·19
                                                        ─────────
                                                        $161,637·38

NOTE. This account shows that portion of the College funds which can be used as a common fund.
The following sums should be deducted from the
amount as belonging to Funds in Trust for Poor
Scholars. John Glover's Annuity - - - 350·00
              William Pennoyer's Annuity - 4,444·44 4,794·44

        Leaving the balance of $148,723·75

INCOME NOT APPLICABLE TO THE EXPENSES OF THE COLLEGE, (Continued.)

FOR PREACHING THE GOSPEL AMONG THE INDIANS - - Cr.

By received of the Massachusetts Hospital Life Insurance Company, one year's Income on $13,000, the principal hereof, to January 1, 1831 - - - - - - - - - $624·00

RECEIVABLE - - - - - - - - - Cr.

By notes and mortgages paid off during the year	- -	58,535·76
" do. in the hands of the Treasurer	304,691·26	
" in the hands of N. I. Bowditch for collection	- 350·00	
		305,041·26
loss on Samuel Norwood's note, settled by compromise	-	28·51
		$363,605·53

LONDON - - - - - - - - - Cr.

By paid for Invoices of Books, and cost of Magazines &c., for the Library - - - -	3,157·17	
" cost of Urn for the late Treasurer - -	318·16	
" balance W. & S. Jones's account - - -	393·00	
Commissions and postages, less Interest, to January 1, 1831 - - - - - -	26·23	
Paid for Invoice of Law Books - - - -	176·28	
" postage to O. Rich, in London - - -	11·21	
		4,082·05
Balance, August 31st, 1831, £135. 11s. 4d. - - -		640·17
		$4,722·22

ACCOUNT - - - - - - - - - Cr.

By Balance, August, 31, 1830 - - - -		159,320·45
" received for sale of College Land in Sedgwick, of J. G. Deane - - - - - - -	348·00	
Less discount on Eastern Money - - -	88	
		347·12
" Amount charged J. G. Deane, Ellsworth, sale of College Lands, but uncollected, in Orleans, - -	50·00	
Bluehill, - -	75·00	
Orland Lot -	75·00	
		200·00
" received a dividend on Shares in former U. S. Bank,	- -	220·00
" increased value of 18 shares in the West Boston Bridge, valued in 1827, at $1,450·19 - - -		1,549·81
		$161,637·38

The following account exhibits the state of the property as embraced and balanced in the Treasurer's books, August 31, 1831. The College Buildings with the Library and other property contained in them belonging to the College, and the Grounds under and adjoining them, have no fixed pecuniary value attached to them in the Treasurer's Books, and are not included in this Account.

Bank Stock, at par, Union Bank	10 shares	1,000·00		
New England Bank	5 "	500 00		
Massachusetts Bank	12 "	3,000·00		
Boston Bank	52 "	2,600·00		
State Bank	60 "	3,000·00		10,100·00
Shares in — Charles River Bridge, 2 shares		2,000·00		
West Boston Bridge 18 "		3,000·00		
Middlesex Canal 1 "		200·00		5,200·00
Notes and Mortgages		304,691·26		
In hands N. I. Bowditch for collection		350·00		
Suspended Notes, payable by annual instalments		2,960·00		308,001·26
Real Estate, Houses and Lands in Cambridge		36,182·20		
Wharf in Cambridge		2,564·10		
Estate in Charlestown		2,603·50		
Printing Office, Cambridge		2,395·64		
Webb Estate, Boston		25,000·00		
Rogers Farm, Waltham, balance of value		3,000 00		
Ward's Island, Boston Harbour		1,200·00		
Coggan's Marsh, Chelsea		1,250·00		
Pews in Meeting-House, Cambridge		410·00		
Reversion in 5 stone buildings on Brattle-Street, at expiration of lease		1,000·00		75,605·44
Property in Books, formerly printed by the College		1,000·00		
Wood,		750·00		
Text Books or Class Books		3,434·61		5,184·61
Debts and Balances.				
Due from Prentiss Mellen, Esq. for Eastern Lands sold, when collected		182.56		
John G. Deane, Esq. do. do. do.		200·00		
Balance with Baring, Brothers, & Co. London		640·17		
do. due from the Law Library		3,485·01		
do. from O. Sparhawk, Steward, term bills, not due,		5,005·29		9,513·03
Annuities, a part are appropriated for special objects.				
Charles River Bridge Annuity of $666·67, half of which is now paid by the Warren Bridge Corporation, has been valued in the Books as a principal of		11,111·11		
West Boston Bridge Annuity, at same amount,		11,111·11		
John Glover's perpetual Annuity of $16·67		350·00		
John Nugate's perpetual Annuity of $16·67		350·00		
William Pennoyer's Annuity in England		4,444·44		27,366·66
Doubtful and Desperate Debts, the value of which now is nothing, and the College property is really minus their amount; they are old debts				4,103·52
	Amount forward,			$445,074·52

		Amount forward,	$445,074·52
Trustees of Count Rumford in Paris, value of amount in their hands belonging to Count Rumford's Legacy		- - -	4,000·00
Deposites with the Massachusetts Hospital Life Insurance Company, a part of which are funds in Reversion, a part in Trust, and a part an Accumulating Fund		- - -	34,973·45
In Reversion, amount to the debit of Trustees of John McLean for his Donation bequeathed in trust, with a reversion to the College on the death of his Widow		- - - -	25,000·00
			$509,047·97

AND THE FOREGOING PROPERTY &c. REPRESENTS THE FOLLOW-
ING FUNDS AND BALANCES, AND IS ANSWERABLE FOR THE
SAME, VIZ.

COLLEGE FUNDS.

Balance of Stock account, the common fund of the College,
    Doubtful and Desperate Debts to be deducted - - 148,723·75

Funds towards Salaries and Grants.
Appropriations for Professors	-	11,506·67	
John Alford's Legacy	- -	26,427·28	
Nicholas Boylston's Legacy	-	26,988·00	
Thomas Cotton's Donation	-	140·00	
Dr. John Cummings's Legacy	-	1,666·66	
Sarah Derby's Legacy	- -	3,639·31	
Abiel Smith's Legacy	-	22,037·93	
Major William Erving's Legacy	-	3,333·34	
Henry Flint's Legacy	-	311·11	
Dr. Ezekiel Hersey's Legacy	-	7,952·00	
Dr. Abner Hersey's Legacy	-	1,666·66	
Jonathan Mason's Legacy	-	550·00	
Esther Sprague's Legacy	- -	1,752·50	
Samuel Eliot's Donation	- -	20,590·00	
Count Rumford's Legacy	-	23,064·99	
			151,626·45

Funds towards Library.
Library Fund	- - -	6,000·00		
William Breed's Legacy (balance)		718·69	6,718·69	
				307,068·89

Funds Accumulating for various purposes.
Fund for Permanent Tutors, including West Boston Bridge Annuity	26,578·14	
Panorama of Athens, including deposite with Hospital Life Ins. Company	908·68	
Ward N. Boylston's Fund for Museum	5,262·10	
do. do. for Books, to Museum account	550·00	
		33,298·92

Funds for Theological purposes.
Balance due Theological Institution	15,202·60	
" of Subscription fund for Pulpit Eloquence and Pastoral Carep	- 8,866·16	
Samuel Dexter's Legacy	- - 6,004·31	
Thomas Cary's Legacy	- 2,274·42	
Samuel Parkman's Donation	- 3,517·75	
George Partridge's Donation	- 2,268·94	38,134·18

                     Amounts forward, $71,433·10 $307,068·89

COLLEGE FUNDS, (Continued.)
Amounts forward $71,433·10 307,068·69

Funds for the Law Department.
 Isaac Royall's Legacy - - - 7,943·63
 Nathan Dane's Donation - - 10,000·00
              17,943·63
Professorship of Natural History } balance of
And Botanic Garden Estate   } this fund   11,456·64
Thomas Hollis's Appropriation for Treasurer - 520·00
                  101,353·37

FUNDS IN TRUST FOR VARIOUS PURPOSES, VIZ.
 Paul Dudley's Legacy on Deposite with Hospital
  Life Insurance Company, $444·44, and Income to
  January 1, 1831 - - - - - - 465·77
 Funds for assisting Poor Scholars, viz.
  Exhibitions (a consolidated fund) - 17,230·33
  Seniors' Exhibitions - 1,200·00
  John Glover's Annuity - - 350·00
  William Pennoyer's Legacy in England 4,444·44
  Mary Saltonstall's Legacy and Income 2,730·00
  Joanna Alford's Legacy and Income 525·00
             26,479·77

For Prizes.
 James Bowdoin's Legacy - - 4,384·39
 W. N. Boylston's for Elocution - 1,065·00
  do. Medical - - 250·00
 Edward Hopkins's for Books - - 294·49
            5,993·88
Sarah Winslow's Donation - - - - 4,769·55
Rev. Daniel Williams's Legacy, deposite with Hospital Life Insurance Company - - - 13,000·00
                50,708·97

FUNDS IN REVERSION TO THE COLLEGE, VIZ.
 John McLean's Donation, in hands of his Trustees 25,000·00
 James Perkins's Donation, deposited with Hospital
  Life Insurance Company - - - - 20,000·00

 Christopher Gore's Donation, deposited with Hospital Life Insurance Company - - - 751·00
                45,751·00
NOTE. Residue of this Donation not ascertained.

Balances, to T. W. Ward, Treasurer - - 31·70
   to Suffolk Bank, checks overdrawn - 4,134·04
               4,165·74
               $509,047·97

COLLEGE PROPERTY NOT PRODUCING A DIRECT INCOME, AND NOT INCLUDED IN THE FOREGOING STATEMENT, AND TO WHICH NO VALUATION IS AFFIXED IN THE COLLEGE BOOKS.

COLLEGE BUILDINGS, and Land under and adjoining, viz.

    Massachusetts Hall.
    Harvard Hall.
    Hollis Hall.
    Stoughton Hall.
    Holworthy Hall.
    Holden Chapel.
    University Hall.
    President's House.
    Medical College, (Boston.)

COLLEGE LIBRARY.
    per Catalogue.

    Law Library.
    Theological Library.
    Medical Library.

Pictures and Statuary,	per Inventory.
Philosophical Apparatus,	per "
Chemical Apparatus,	per "
Anatomical Preparations and Museum	per "
Minerals and Fossils,	per "
Furniture and Utensils	per "

Botanic Garden Estate.
Divinity Hall Estate.
Matron's House and Furniture.
Eastern Lands, of uncertain but of supposed small value.